Kid-Tested Writing Lessons

for Grades 3–6

Daily Workshop Practices That Support the Common Core State Standards

Leslie Blauman

HEINEMANN
Portsmouth, NH

Heinemann
361 Hanover Street
Portsmouth, NH 03801–3912
www.heinemann.com

Offices and agents throughout the world

The author and publisher wish to thank those who have generously given permission to reprint borrowed material:

Excerpts from *Common Core State Standards*. © Copyright 2010. National Governors Association Center for Best Practices and Council of Chief State School Officers. All rights reserved.

Figures I.2 and 2.1: Excerpts from *Colorado Nature Almanac. A Month-By-Month Guide to Wildlife and Wild Places* by Stephen R. Jones and Ruth Carol Cushman. Copyright © 1998. Published by Pruett Publishing Company. Reprinted by permission of the publisher and authors.

Library of Congress Cataloging-in-Publication Data
Blauman, Leslie.
   Kid-tested writing lessons for grades 3–6 : daily workshop practices that support the common core state standards / Leslie Blauman.
        p. cm.
   Includes bibliographical references and index.
   ISBN-13: 978-0-325-04166-7
   ISBN-10: 0-325-04166-0
   1. English language—Composition and exercises—Study and teaching (Elementary)—United States.   2. Education, Elementary—Standards—United States—States.   I. Title.
   LB1576.B4984 2012
   372.6'044—dc23   2011043542

Editor: Tobey Antao
Acquiring editor: Wendy Murray
Developmental editor: Alan Huisman
Production: Victoria Merecki
Interior and cover designs: Monica Crigler
Photographer: Barry Staver
Typesetter: Publishers' Design & Production Services, Inc.
Manufacturing: Steve Bernier

Printed in the United States of America on acid-free paper
16   15   14   13   12   VP   1   2   3   4   5

Dedication

In loving memory of my father,
Austin A. Burch

Contents

Lesson Cluster Four
Writing Nonfiction: Getting Beyond the Five-Paragraph Theme   156

Foreword

It is the first day of a new year and I have just finished reading *Kid-Tested Writing Lessons*. As I put down the manuscript and pick up my pen, I feel a sense of new beginnings and celebration. I can't help but smile as I picture Leslie's classroom (a lively, invigorating place where children read, write, talk, and share as they take charge of their learning) and reflect on how miraculously she has captured that energy on the page. Friendly, welcoming, a bit sassy (this is a lady who wears spiked heels every day in her classroom), Leslie presents us with a new way of being in the classroom: a way that releases teachers from the tyranny of tests and administrivia and reminds them why they chose to do what they do and why it is essential to the well-being and growth of children. Through these lessons, she shows how she gets kids to think—not simply parrot what they believe she wants them to say or write but push their intellectual envelope and grapple with ideas, all in elementary school! Leslie takes her work seriously, but despite that seriousness she makes it fun—and rewarding—for children. Learning *is* fun when children are allowed to explore and make sense of the remarkable world around them, when they have the freedom to select books they want to read and topics they want to research, when they set off on a journey of expansion and under-standing. The path Leslie blazes here opens enthralling vistas and possibilities.

In many ways, this is a book about love: love of children, love of learning, love of teaching, love of words, love of the power of literature, love of reading, love of writing, love of this exquisite planet Earth. Leslie shares her passion, her caring, her high standards with her students every day. She lets them know, in no uncertain terms, that each of them has the potential to be a real writer and a real reader. No one is off the hook. She cares about them and believes in their intelligence and abilities. A masterful coach, she brings out the best in each of her "athletes," and she shows them—and you—exactly how to do it. Leslie is the chief scholar in her classroom. Though she would never call herself that or even think of herself that way, she is. She is not just the chief teacher; she is the chief learner. She writes along with her students; reads tons of books; pays attention; asks questions; pursues interests; listens; goes deeper; and keeps learning. Leslie is an amazing teacher, but she doesn't intimidate, she elevates, both her students and other teachers.

There are numerous revelations here: the importance of giving students choice and responsibility so that they "own" their work; the importance of creating and nurturing a community of thinkers; the importance of reading a lot and writing a lot and making the time to practice sacred. But there is another revelation that is absolutely key yet frequently overlooked or ignored, especially in elementary school. To teach writing well, there is only one place to go: to great writers who have mastered the craft. It makes perfect sense. Leslie figured this out a long time ago. She doesn't go to work sheets or to formulaic programs. She depends instead on the brilliance and teaching power of "mentor texts," superbly written books, poems, articles, editorials, and essays. She provides lists of them in each chapter and takes you step by step through how she uses them with her students. With marvelous texts in hand, Leslie and her students study word choice, turns of phrase, description, characterization, plot, leads, and endings from the best writing teachers out there, excellent authors. Through this process, they increase their vocabulary, analyze quality writing, explore how to make nonfiction come alive, experience great minds at work, all the while building critical background knowledge. Leslie's students learn not only how to write well but how to read better, with more focus and care. They read with a writer's eye. They write with a reader's eye. They come to see that reading and writing are fundamentally connected, a dance in which it takes two to tango—the writing reinforces the reading, the reading reinforces the writing.

It's been a tough time in education. Budget cuts have led to layoffs throughout the country. High-stakes testing has put enormous pressure on teachers to teach to the test. Teachers often feel under fire and deal with high anxiety and worry about how they can fit *everything* into their days. A mantra of rush, rush, rush overtakes classrooms. This book is an antidote to that fast-paced, over-programmed, crazed classroom in which children rarely have time to process what they are learning and explore real passions and interests. There is nothing packaged about the lessons Leslie outlines here. Each one is thoughtful, challenging, and deliberate. Each one builds on what came before. Each one focuses on how to make students independent, capable, writers (and readers) who have learned at the feet of the greats. Presented in a user-friendly fashion that allows teachers to choose exactly what will most support them where they are, each lesson also ties to the Common Core State Standards (CCSS), showing how thoughtful, in-depth thinking and real writing are what is expected under CCSS. You simply can't fake it!

For twenty-five years I have visited Leslie's classroom. It has always been an extraordinary place where children are challenged, where passions are pursued and explorations encouraged. What has changed is that Leslie has become more intentional. She knows exactly why she does what she does. She has studied it, thought about it, tested it on children over the years. She knows what works and what doesn't. She knows how to engage children, even the most reluctant student. She began with natural talent. She has broken it down and honed it to extraordinary mastery. In this book she shares lesson after lesson from her wealth of experience, all kid-tested. This is a how-to book with a twist; not only does she break down what she has done over many years in her classroom, sharing what she has learned, what works and what doesn't, but she shows you how to make it yours. She sets you off on the journey but knows that as with her students, she can't take that journey for you. You must do it on your own—with a little help from a friend.

Susan Zimmermann
Coauthor of *Mosaic of Thought* and *7 Keys to Comprehension*

And then Smokey Daniels. He truly is my mentor. What an author! I use so much of his work in my own teaching. Brilliant. Then to get him as an editor? How lucky can you get! He also brought an angle to this book, and always with humor! He will always be "Uncle Smokey"! Thank you—for working on this, and for influencing me as a teacher.

The rest of the Heinemann family. Alan Huisman. I said I couldn't do this book without Alan. Every author needs an editor like Alan, with an eye and a true understanding of writing. His polish and expertise makes any author look brilliant. So, Alan, thank you for taking the uncut version and polishing it into a gem. You're the best!

Vicki Kasabian laid the groundwork on the production of this book and then Victoria Merecki took over. She has been a terrific production editor and has taken the written text and turned it into a book that I'm proud of. Thank you for your vision!

To Sarah Fournier, who kept me organized! To Barry Staver, for taking amazing photos of my students to include in this book. You were so patient with an author who absolutely hates having photos taken! To Elizabeth Valway, for promotion. To Cindy Ann Black, for final edits. To Lisa Fowler, Vice-President of Design and Production, who designed *The Inside Guide*, and to Monica Crigler, who took her work and ran with it for this book. I love the design! Thank you all!

Families. Another of my families is the PEBC. This book evolved from my work with the PEBC. My mentors, my friends—the people I look up to. Susan Zimmermann started me on this journey. Truly an amazing woman and a visionary. She has touched so many children by starting the PEBC! Besides touching children's lives, you have impacted so many people—teachers especially—through your words and your actions. You have truly been a mentor to me, and I cannot thank you enough for writing such a beautiful foreword. Thank you does not even begin to capture how touched I am. I am the teacher I am today because of what you started.

Chryse Hutchins knows my classroom better than anyone. Without her scripts and her nudges, her "Leslie, you have to include this in your book," I wouldn't have been able to truly capture my classroom. Stephanie Harvey is my mentor. Her name appears throughout this book. Her influence on my teaching and my thinking has been instrumental. To all the other wise and wonderful folks at the PEBC and the authors I cite here, I thank you, and my students thank you. The best is that we continue to learn.

My kids. My students. This is your book. These are the lessons you told me mattered. These are your stories. Your thinking. Your brilliance. You know I love you, and you know how amazed I was every time you shared your thinking or your writing. Many students are represented on these pages , but *all* of you could have your words, your writing, your thinking, included here. But I have to give a special call out to you, Maddie, because you lead us into this book. The story I start with is true (Chryse Hutchins captured it verbatim). And it is totally Maddie. Thank you for helping me explain how powerful writing can be! And thanks to all the students I've taught over the years. Yes, I remember all of you! (And I hope you're writing!)

My school family. I have taught in many schools, and I'm fortunate to work in schools across the country and outside the U.S. as a consultant. I'm amazed at what teachers are doing for our students. I'm proud to be a teacher. But I have to also say that I work with one of the most dedicated, talented staffs there is. To all the teachers at Cherry Hills Elementary School—the children are lucky to have you. And I especially want to thank my teammates: Jessica Ehrlich, Kristin Schultz, Kelly Kirby, and Christine Rucks. I love teaching with you and learning with you. To say you are amazing is an understatement.

I also want to thank our special services team. These are "the best of the best," teachers who work with children who need support. The support they offer to teachers and the growth they elicit from students is incredible. And always with humor and love. Sue Beman, Lauren Myers, and Carolyn Moore, thank you for what you do for both students and teachers. You are amazing. But even more important, the students love you. What else can I say except, can we clone you?

Principals. They allow us to teach. We need to say thank you to our principals when they are exemplary. They are under a lot of pressure these days in this educational environment, and deserve our thanks! In *The Inside Guide* I thanked all the principals that have helped shape me as a teacher. Principals have power, and when you work for great ones, it's amazing what can happen at a school. And I've worked with some wonderful principals. I've taught a long time, but I want to say thank you to two of the most recent principals who have made a difference in the school, the teachers, and most important the children. Trina Rich was a true visionary. And now we have Molly Drevenkar, who uses the metaphor that we are all "on the boat." She is a phenomenal captain and is steering the boat in the right direction. It is a joy to be "on the boat" with her!

Special thanks to Bev Robin, who shares the power of the written word through her vocabulary work in *Empowering Words*—you help us stretch and extend our students. To the entire staff at The Bookies, a truly exceptional book store in Denver. Any time I venture in I leave with more books than anticipated, but the staff always steers me toward books that will enrich my classroom. Every city needs a special bookstore like this, and I have to mention it, because mentor texts are front and center in this book.

True friends. Friends who support. Who wait. Who encourage. Another family. Sue Beman, Kate Blanchard, Trina Rich, Trina Hayden, Lauren Myers—you are my "Ya Ya's girls" and I love you.

To Cathy Viotta, my trainer and friend. You keep me balanced and always remind me to be mindful. I am lucky to work with you and laugh with you. You keep me focused.

To my muse. You asked me to tell you. Of course I do. I always have. I always will. And I love how you influence my writing. Thank you.

And finally, to my own family. My mom. My mother, Alice Burch, knows the power of the written word and instilled that love in me. I love you, Mom. My brother, Andy Burch—I do words, you do music. You never cease to amaze me! And Jill (another teacher) and Allison and Mark, my niece and nephew. I won't be surprised if I see Allison or Mark published one day! You both are incredibly talented, and I'm proud of you.

My two. I always end with you, don't I? Because you have to save the best for last. My daughter, Carolynn, and my son, John. Being your mom is the best role in the world. I am proud of the people you've grown up to be. I can't wait to see where life takes you. I am so incredibly proud of you and I love you more than words can say (and whew, since this is a book on writing, that's saying a lot!).

But finally, back to Dad—or as my children called him, "Hop Pop"—I hope you're proud. I was lucky to have you as my father. I miss you terribly and I really do hope you're smiling!

Introduction

Whenever and wherever you read this, picture a cold, snowy day in Denver, Colorado, in January. My fourth graders and I spend the morning reading and writing. Toward the end of the workshop, we read a descriptive piece on January from the *Colorado Nature Almanac*, by Stephen R. Jones and Ruth Carol Cushman (1998). Students then do a quick-write.

When they finish, Maddie volunteers to read hers aloud (Figure I.1):

January

Mounds of snow sit in ditches, as the wind brushes up the glistening snow and turns into eddies. Bears wake up and stretch, getting ready to give birth to little ones. The New Year has draped its coat in the closet and settled in. The trees still stand all skinny with twigs, the snow carpets the glazed ground. King Winter's gift has danced down from the spongy clouds. Only tufts of grass stand straight up with a necklace of dew pearls.

▶ THE NITTY GRITTY

The PEBC was started over twenty-five years ago to bridge the gap between the private sector and the public schools. The PEBC spearheaded numerous projects to increase community involvement and improve the quality of public education in the Denver metro area. Early on, it began a staff development initiative focused on quality writing instruction, specifically writing workshops. That focus quickly grew and expanded to include strategies that proficient readers use. The PEBC has been instrumental in shaping me as a literacy teacher, allowing me to work with the "best of the best," and I share my learning with you in this book.

As her teacher, I know her literary influences. The words *glistening* and *eddies* in her first sentence are drawn from the first paragraph of the piece we just read (see her annotations to the first page in Figure I.2). The bear detail comes from our study of Colorado animals. The imagery of the trees piggybacks Rylant's *In November* (Sandpiper, 2000). However, the rest is Maddie—and her last sentence is an absolute and wonderful surprise.

That day, educators participating in a Public Education and Business Coalition (PEBC) National Lab are visiting our classroom. When Maddie finishes, one of them says, "Wow. How did you do that?"

Figure I.1 Maddie's Quick-Write from her Writer's Notebook

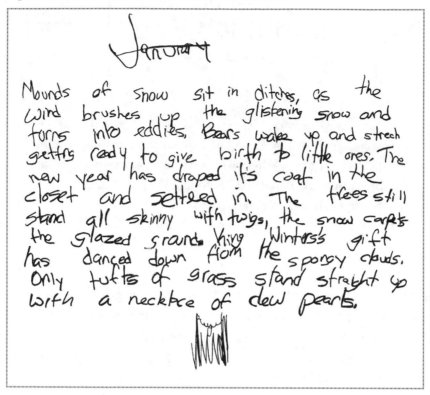

Maddie smiles, pulls out her writer's folder, and shows them the Rylant piece and other mentor texts. Just as I am able to identify her influences, Maddie knows them too. The visitors are still curious, so she takes them out in the hall to show them other examples of student writing, stopping to point out our writing anchor charts that exemplify beautiful language. She explains how these, too, influenced her writing, gave her the immersion in craft that enabled her to write her piece in ten minutes.

The visitors push to know more, the alchemy of it.

"We study mentor texts a lot," Maddie says, "and we do reading and writing together."

Later, when the visitors and I gather for a debriefing conversation, I tell them that Maddie's writing reflects all the practices I describe in *The Inside Guide to the Reading–Writing Classroom, Grades 3–6: Strategies for Extraordinary Teaching* (2011)—the foundational lessons, the creation of anchor charts, the minilessons and conferences, the mesh of reading and writing study and practice

Figure I.2 Maddie's Coding

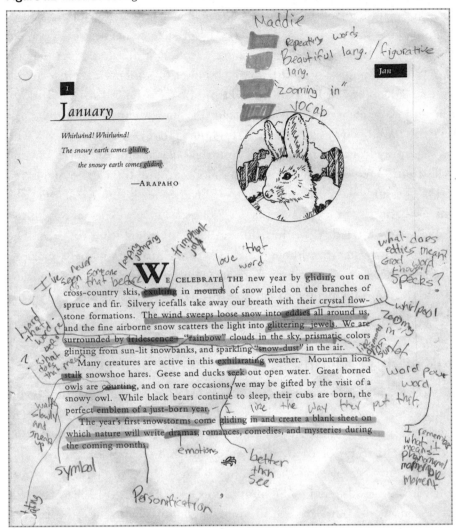

in our workshop. I interlace the fingers of each hand to symbolize this integrated instruction.

Why do visiting educators observe my instruction? Why am I writing a book of writing lessons? Who am I to offer advice?

I was fortunate to "grow up" with the PEBC, having teacher trainers in my room, reading and studying and growing with some of the best mentors: Ellin Oliver Keene, Susan Zimmermann, Stephanie Harvey, Anne Goudvis, Chryse Hutchins, Lori Conrad, Patrick Allen, Bruce Morgan, Debbie Miller…the list is long. These are my friends and colleagues.

The question visiting teachers ask year after year—"How did you get the kids this far?"—pushed me into writing. I'm a teacher first and foremost. I've taught kindergarten through sixth grade. I've taught in schools with a 75 percent mobility rate, high poverty, and little support. I've taught in middle class schools that have morphed into schools with a large number of students learning English as a second language. Students in my classroom have had Russian, Turkish, Spanish, and Korean as their first language. I've taught in rooms with many children who have been designated gifted and talented. I've taught students who are one step away from the behaviorally disturbed classroom. Although I'm still in the classroom, I now consult and work in schools around the United States and the world. The students in these schools have diverse needs, but *I teach literacy the same way. Always.* I may change the level of text, but my expectations always remain high. And the kids perform. Kids are kids, and they want to learn. The bottom line—I love to teach. Although I enjoy writing and working with teachers, my heart is in the classroom and my students know that. And, like Maddie, they want to share what's happening in our room. That's the opportunity I'm giving you. Come in and sit down; we want you to eavesdrop!

A Look at the Lessons

In this book I share the writing lessons that year after year are the kids' favorites—the lessons that the students, boys *and* girls, consistently say make them better writers. Just as Maddie shared with our visitors how she wrote her piece, my students, at the end of each year, share with me what books and lessons have made the most impact on their writing. That's what I'm giving you—over twenty-five years of kid-tested, kid-approved lessons. These lessons lead to great writing—for authentic purposes *and* in testing situations. Knowing how to write well is a skill that transfers to any situation. Immerse students in great literature and writing—mentor texts—teach them how to write well, and see how far they go! These lessons were developed in a reading and writing workshop, but they are so much about the craft of writing—the inner workings and the inspiration of mentor texts—that they can be used in any classroom context.

To counteract the warp speed and high pressure of education today, I've made this book deliberately simple and spare. There is an ongoing skirmish in professional development circles about whether teachers should take lessons from books and follow them verbatim. I used to squirm at the thought of that too, but I've come to realize the concern is nonsense. I'm a teacher, and I know that the moment a teacher is ready, she will take an example lesson and refine it, trim it down, beef it up, or put it aside. Until that time, what's wrong with a little mentorship? These lessons are generative, springboards to which you'll give your personal stamp.

▶ **THE NITTY GRITTY**

These writing lessons:

- Are kid favorites
- Mirror the books used in reading lessons; incorporate mentor texts
- Support the Common Core State Standards (CCSS)
- Are based on research

These lessons also have deep roots. They reflect my core beliefs and the stances these beliefs engender. They are the sequel to *The Inside Guide to the Reading–Writing Classroom*, and I encourage you to check out that resource for a fuller context. These lessons build on the foundation of that book, are its natural extension. They mirror the reading lessons found there. They bridge the reading and writing workshop and often use the same mentor texts.

How did I settle on just these lessons? If you visited my class, you'd see that I present writing units of study not covered here—every year looks different. I couldn't include everything—I had to be choosey. Which ones did my students say made a difference in their writing? In this high-stakes testing environment, which ones help students do well on tests without violating the integrity of the writing workshop? Which ones align with standards? If I were a beginning teacher, which ones would get me started? These lessons let you start small but with the most important components, the ones that bring power and beauty to your students' writing and to your writing classroom. They do what Maddie said: They focus on mentor texts and interweave reading and writing.

One more thing. The more I study writing and writers, the more I am struck by the fact that we teachers *must write too*. This is often very uncomfortable—writing is hard. But if we are going to teach our children, we have to experience the struggles and triumphs they do. No, you don't have to be a published author. But your kids do need to see you writing. Then they buy in! Try these lessons with your kids and write alongside them. You might be surprised with what you come up with!

How to Use This Book

I love the word *purpose*. It focuses my instruction and focuses my students. *Why? Why are we doing this? Why did you think that or make that particular decision? What is the *purpose* for these lessons and *how* will they improve students' writing? Think of what you need to teach your students in your grade level and then pick and choose from these lessons to meet your *purpose*.

Accountability is another powerful word in education right now. Good instruction matches outcomes, and these lessons mesh with the CCSS, to include those on writing, reading, speaking, and listening. The introductions to each of the four lesson clusters, along with the CCSS Grade by Grade boxes, help you see how the lessons support the CCSS.

The four sections of this book are (1) note taking and the writing process for narratives, informational writing, and argument writing; (2) language study and the writing process for poetry; (3) a unit on writing fiction; and (4) a unit on writing research-based nonfiction.

Some lessons stand on their own. Some work best as part of a group. Some need to be presented in a specific sequence. I'll tell you which are which.

Repeating sections of boxed material that amplifies or explains things in the text include:

- *The Nitty-Gritty:* details, reasons, enhancements
- *The Language of Learning:* language to use in your classroom as well as terms, acronyms, and so on, demystified
- *To Learn More:* resources for more information
- *Using Technology:* ideas/links for incorporating technology

What You Need to Know Before Jumping In
WRITER'S NOTEBOOKS AND BOOK LOVER'S BOOKS

In *The Inside Guide* I write about setting up the year and my thought process before the students set foot in the room. One of the key elements to my reading workshop is the book lover's book—the BLB—in which students capture all their thinking about reading and which bridges the reading and writing workshop. But I also have to plan for writing, not only the writing I want to accomplish in writing workshop, but also writing in the content areas. Many of the lessons in this book support content-area writing. Before each school year, I spend some time in office supply stores noticing new materials that might make my writing instruction more interesting. Yes, there are new pens and containers, and of course technology races on. Yet I always return to the tried-and-true when organizing my writer's workshop supplies. I head to the folders and notebooks.

The materials section of the lessons often lists the writer's notebook. I use a spiral notebook, but any type is fine. And no matter what grade level, some way of keeping loose-leaf papers together is essential. I use pocketed folders, but three-ring binders or other organizers are okay too—whatever works for you and your students.

THE WRITING PROCESS

The writing process is the engine for all we do. In many of the lessons in this book, students use mentor texts to improve their writing. This practice work is done in the writer's notebook, and the pieces may not make their way through the entire writing process. Lesson clusters, on the other hand, take the students through the entire writing process to a final product. The lessons in Cluster One, "Writing Narratives, Informative Texts, and Opinion Pieces: In Pursuit of Paragraphs," introduce the writing process (see Figure I.3).

TO LEARN MORE

The writer's notebook (call it what you want) is the most important tool of my writing workshop. It's the practice book for all the published writing we do. Ralph Fletcher's *A Writer's Notebook: Unlocking the Writer Within You* (1996) is written for kids, but it is chock-full of great advice. I use his analogy of digging for crystals as students peruse their notebooks for nuggets to turn into final pieces: "Your notebook will fill up with lots of intriguing stuff. Imagine your raw notebook material as mineralized rocks you have dragged home. In that rough stone all sorts of agates, crystals, and valuable fossils might be buried. It's up to you to dig them out" (113). He continues, "Reread carefully. And don't expect to find perfectly polished gems all ready for publication because you probably won't . . . instead look for potential, places where you suspect you might have something good if you develop and polish your words" (115).

Other excellent professional books on notebooks are Ralph Fletcher and JoAnn Portalupi's *Writing Workshop: The Essential Guide* (2001), Shelley Harwayne's *Writing Through Childhood: Rethinking Process and Product* (2001), and Linda Rief's *Inside the Writer's-Reader's Notebook: A Workshop Essential* (2007).

- *Planning/envisioning*. The prewriting stage—immersing yourself in similar texts and deciding what the final product wil look like. What other published text will your piece look like? A picture book? A poem? A chapter of a novel? An editorial? Students need to know what they're creating.

- *Drafting*. Getting the words down.

- *Revising*. Looking at the draft with new eyes, adding or deleting text, asking questions. Only for pieces worthy of revision.

Figure I.3 The Writing Process

- [*Writers circle between drafting and revision until the text is the way they want it.*]

- *Editing.* Polishing the grammar and syntax and taking care of the mechanics.

- *Finalizing/going public.* An important part of the process. If kids are only writing for you, what's the point? They need to share their final pieces with a larger audience. (Includes reflections and celebrations.)

TO LEARN MORE

Ruth Culham's *Traits of Writing: The Complete Guide for Middle School* (2010) and Vicki Spandel's *Creating Writers Through 6-Trait Writing Assessment and Instruction* (2000) provide a great foundation. While I was working on this section, I read *Hidden Gems*, by Katherine Bomer (2010). In this wonderful book, Bomer tells how to respond to the positives in kids' writing even when it seems there aren't any. She also shows how to go beyond the six-trait lingo.

THE SIX TRAITS OF WRITING

Of course the six traits share space with the writing process in that we arc aware of these qualities of writing from the get-go and of how attending to them can strengthen our writing. There has been a great deal written lately about the value of using these traits in classrooms as a be-all, end-all writing assessment. I use them as a start, but I always add written comments in response to student work. (See Figure I.4.)

Okay. Now it's time for me, like Maddie, to walk you through our favorite lessons from a school year. Pick and choose and see what works for you—and watch your kids write!

TO LEARN MORE

Graves, Donald. 1994. *A Fresh Look at Writing*. Portsmouth, NH: Heinemann.

Ray, Katie Wood. 1999. *Wondrous Words*. Urbana, IL: National Council of Teachers of English.

Ray, Katie Wood, with Lester Laminack. 2001. *The Writing Workshop: Working Through the Hard Parts (And They're All Hard Parts)*. Urbana, IL: National Council of Teachers of English.

Figure I.4 Ruth Culham's Six Traits of Writing

The Six Traits of Writing (as Presented in *Traits of Writing*, by Ruth Culham 2010)
Ideas: the piece's content—its central message and the details that support that message
Organization: the internal structure of the piece—the thread of logic, the pattern of learning
Voice: the tone and tenor of the piece—the personal stamp of the writer, achieved through a strong understanding of purpose and audience
Word choice: the vocabulary the writer uses to convey meaning and enlighten the reader
Sentence fluency: the way words and phrases flow through the piece
Conventions: the mechanical correctness of the piece—spelling, capitalization, punctuation, paragraphing, grammar, and usage—that guides the reader through the text and makes it easy to follow

Writing Narratives, Informative Texts, and Opinion Pieces

In Pursuit of Paragraphs

1. Envisioning, Planning, and Note Taking: Immersing Ourselves in Our Topic
2. Drafting: Shaping Our Ideas
3. Revising: Looking at Our Work with New Eyes
4. Editing: Polishing Our Writing
5. Finalizing: Taking Our Work Public

For some teachers, *writing workshop* means immersing students in the warm bath of fiction and poetry; content writing is often overlooked. I put content writing front and center. At the beginning of the year, I present a basic weeklong lesson cluster on using the writing process and writing across the curriculum. The lessons, each building on the previous one, establish a structure for successful writing; many are directly connected to later lessons in this book.

Crafting "President Paragraphs"

All students need to be able to craft paragraphs. Paragraphs are the backbone of organization. Well-written paragraphs move a reader through a piece effortlessly; kids have to write them and write them *well*. They have to know the difference between *narrative, descriptive, expository*, and *persuasive* writing to do well on standardized tests. That's life.

1

However, I am not in favor of templates, so I use paragraphs to teach both skills and beautiful writing and move on. Once students understand how to construct narrative, descriptive (informative/explanatory), and persuasive (opinion) paragraphs, they can accomplish the rich content writing on which I focus the rest of the year.

Every student in my classroom has a weekly job. These jobs (discussed in more detail in Chapter 6, pages 161–63, of *The Inside Guide to the Reading–Writing Classroom*) help our classroom move smoothly and foster independence. One of these jobs is classroom president. This job carries a lot of responsibility; just as the president runs the country, our classroom president runs the classroom. For example, she or he forms and leads the line when we leave the classroom for lunch or any other reason, greets adults who enter our room, and checks to make sure students' homework planners have been signed (but does not monitor student behavior). Every student is president at least once during the year, and the students love the status and expectations it entails.

During their week as president, students are interviewed by the class. Each president comes prepared to share at least two stories and details of his or her family, interests, and passions. Class members learn a lot about their classmates, I learn a lot about my students, and we get to eliminate "show and tell." The interviews are a powerful way to build community. When Heather shared the hardships she has faced, our eyes were opened to how difficult people's lives can be. When Yuri, a student from South Korea, was able to tell her stories *in English* in the spring, we were amazed and supportive.

Even better, these stories and details are fodder for the paragraphs the students write. I use the stories to teach *narrative* writing; the details to teach *descriptive* and *informative* writing; and students' passions, interests, and strengths to teach *persuasive* (opinion) writing. These "president paragraphs" span the year, but in the early weeks they help me teach and demonstrate the writing process. And once we've learned how to write powerful paragraphs, we can turn our attention to the wide array of writing!

As you read this cluster of lessons, think how you would use president paragraphs to *demonstrate* the writing process to your students. What types of writing are you accountable for teaching at your grade level? Narrative, descriptive, persuasive? How much writing do you require a week? Figure 1.1 is an example of what a week of president paragraphs looks like in my classroom.

I want my students to have lots of practice writing authentically for informal and formal assessments. The key word is *authentically*. My students would be

Figure 1.1 A Weeklong View of Our Work with President Paragraphs

PRESIDENT PARAGRAPHS				
Monday	**Tuesday**	**Wednesday**	**Thursday**	**Friday**
Interview president and take two-column notes; as homework, begin drafting	Draft (often at home)	Revise (in class)	Edit (in class) and work on final copies (in class and at home)	Turn in final copies

the first to tell you that they do not like writing to prompts; they're boring. When they're learning about their classmates, there is an engaged quality to the writing. More importantly, I can say unequivocally that this practice transfers to tests that require writing. My students know what to do and how they will be scored (remember, no surprises).

Aligning Your Instruction with the Common Core State Standards

The lessons in this book are kid-tested, kid-approved: They help my students write better, and students overwhelmingly tell me they love to write because of these lessons. That's my line in the sand. I teach kids how to write authentically.

THE LANGUAGE OF LEARNING

No surprises is a key mandate in my classroom. When students understand the purpose and the expectations—and how they're doing in relation to those expectations—their work improves. Trust and honesty allow kids to take risks. And when they take risks in their learning, the sky's the limit. Before we start, I show the students the grading criteria or the rubric that will be used. And as I confer with students, I'm honest about how I view them as a reader and a writer. From day 1, I tell the kids they may ask me anything except very private questions (like my weight!) and I will answer them truthfully. And because I'm the first storyteller, I can scaffold the process—and the kids get to learn a lot about me!

If students know how to write—and write well—that knowledge will transfer to testing and other situations. Kids just need to know purpose and audience.

So how do the Common Core State Standards (CCSS) fit in? I think you'll find, as I did, that the CCSS reflect real writing; they're not an "add-on" to what we already do in our literacy classrooms but perhaps a different way of labeling what we do. We need to know these standards, because we're accountable for teaching them.

In this lesson cluster, students learn to write different types of texts, learn the writing process, and take pieces to completion (finalize them and share them with an audience). The lessons address the following standards:

COLLEGE AND CAREER READINESS ANCHOR STANDARDS FOR WRITING

TEXT TYPES AND PURPOSES

1. Write arguments to support claims in an analysis of substantive topics or texts, using valid reasoning and relevant and sufficient evidence.

2. Write informative/explanatory texts to examine and convey complex ideas and information clearly and accurately through the effective selection, organization, and analysis of content.

3. Write narratives to develop real or imagined experiences or events using effective technique, well-chosen details, and well-structured event sequences.

In these lessons students learn how to write paragraphs of all these types of texts, knowledge that then transfers to longer pieces. Text types and purposes are dealt with throughout the lessons in this book.

PRODUCTION AND DISTRIBUTION OF WRITING

4. Produce clear and coherent writing in which the development, organization, and style are appropriate to task, purpose, and audience.

5. Develop and strengthen writing as needed by planning, revising, editing, rewriting, or trying a new approach.

6. Use technology, including the Internet, to produce and publish writing and to interact and collaborate with others.

The writing process is embedded in these standards, and the lessons in this cluster teach the writing process. All writers write to specific audiences, and purpose is always important (why are we doing this?). Students publish and share their work, and technology (*what would we do without word processing?*) is an integral part of classrooms and publication.

RANGE OF WRITING

7. Write routinely over extended time frames (time for research, reflection, and revision) and shorter time frames (a single sitting or a day or two) for a range of tasks, purposes, and audiences.

In these lessons writers park themselves in their chair (or at their desk) and stick with it. It becomes a habit. The more kids write, the longer they can stick with it. Great writing doesn't happen in one sitting. It takes time.

COLLEGE AND CAREER READINESS ANCHOR STANDARDS FOR LANGUAGE

CONVENTIONS OF STANDARD ENGLISH

8. Demonstrate command of the conventions of standard English grammar and usage when writing or speaking.

9. Demonstrate command of the conventions of standard English capitalization, punctuation, and spelling when writing.

Lesson 4 in this section addresses the conventions of standard English. So often in writing, the conventions, not the content, are evaluated. By attending to conventions at the end of the writing process, students 'finish' their writing so that it's ready to go public. They learn how to use the conventions in an authentic manner.

COLLEGE AND CAREER READINESS ANCHOR STANDARDS FOR SPEAKING AND LISTENING

COMPREHENSION AND COLLABORATION

10. Prepare for and participate effectively in a range of conversations and collaborations with diverse partners, building on others' ideas and expressing their own clearly and persuasively.

During students' time as president, they share two stories with the class orally. The rest of the class listens for details and takes notes. In addition, students have meaningful conversations throughout these lessons. They confer with others and share their thinking. Seeking feedback from others is an authentic part of the writing process.

PRESENTATION OF KNOWLEDGE AND IDEAS

11. Present information, findings, and supporting evidence such that listeners can follow the line of reasoning, and the organization, development, and style are appropriate to task, purpose, and audience.

12. Make strategic use of digital media and visual displays of data to express information and enhance understanding of presentations.

13. Adapt speech to a variety of contexts and communicative tasks, demonstrating command of formal English when indicated or appropriate.

When students are president, they learn to share rich, detailed, organized stories about their lives.

Lesson 1

Envisioning, Planning, and Note Taking

Immersing Ourselves in Our Topic

(day 1 of 5)

Introduction

This lesson focuses on planning (practicing, rehearsing, and envisioning). Students gather information to use in drafting president paragraphs. They also learn how to take two-column notes separating the main idea and the details, a skill used in all content areas through their remaining years in school and later in their lives and careers.

Because I am the first president of the classroom, I model being interviewed. As I share stories and information about my life, I take notes for students to copy. (If you have a blog, you can post the notes there for students to access later.) Students remain at their desks (as long as they can see the board), and I encourage them to ask questions throughout the interview.

MENTOR TEXTS FOR STUDENTS

The list below includes just a few titles of picture books that are representative of the kinds of stories we tell. They are good examples of "zooming in" on specific events to help the reader visualize and understand the importance of the story.

- Marion Dane Bauer's *When I Go Camping with Grandma* (Troll Communications, 1995)
- Pat Brisson's *The Summer My Father Was 10* (Boyds Mills, 1998)

- Sandra Cisneros's *The House on Mango Street* (Vintage, 1989)
- Gloria Houston's *My Great-Aunt Arizona* (HarperCollins, 1997)
- Helen Ketteman's *I Remember Papa* (Puffin, 1998)
- Cynthia Rylant's *The Relatives Came* (Live Oak Media, 1999)
- James Stevenson's *When I Was Nine* (Greenwillow, 1986)
- Myron Uhlberg's *Dad, Jackie, and Me* (Peachtree, 2010)
- Jane Yolen's *Owl Moon* (Philomel, 1987)

MATERIALS

- Spiral notebooks (students). Students keep a second spiral notebook (in addition to their writer's notebook), called a *president notebook*.
- Overhead projector or document camera or SMART Board (teacher).

TIME: Approximately 45 minutes

▶ **THE NITTY-GRITTY**

When I first introduced president paragraphs, I had students take notes and write their drafts in their writer's notebook. However, that was cumbersome; students were flipping through their notebook for paragraphs and for other writing projects. So I started using separate notebooks.

Here's How It Goes

"All of you have your president notebooks out—these are where we'll take notes and do our drafting. Would you please open up to your first page and write at the top *Mrs. Blauman*.

"Then I want you to make two columns; but watch what I do first. I want the column on the left to be thinner than the one on the right. We're going to do more writing in the one on the right. Then label these *main idea* and *details*. I organize my thoughts before I start so that my notes will be grouped around main ideas." As I'm explaining, I'm modeling on the document camera.

"I'm going to start out by telling several stories. You guys will be telling stories, too. I'll expect you to share two stories. So what we're going to do in the notes is write down *Story 1, The Dog Lady* in the main idea column, and I'm going to share a story about my time in Alaska and why I love dogs so much. As I tell the story, do you have to write it down exactly the way I tell it, or do you write important information to help you remember? Well, it's more important to listen attentively. You can use abbreviations; just catch the important information."

I tell the students about my time in Craig, Alaska, right after I graduated from college. As I tell the story (and I include rich details), I take quick notes. (See Figure 1.2.) Then I give the kids time to catch up and ask me questions (not make connections), and I add my answers in the detail section.

I follow this story with another on Bandit's encounter with a porcupine and then one on catching sea turtle eggs in Cancun. I choose stories that allow students to catch a glimpse of me as a person, not a teacher.

After that, I describe myself and my passions and interests. "I'm going to share about my family first, because they are incredibly important to me. And I'm going to share about what I like to do when I'm not with you. You know I love to teach, but I do other things too." Figure 1.3 is an example of the notes that capture what I share. Kids may ask questions throughout, but it's a time for them to get to know me as more than a teacher. (And it's a huge factor in building trust.)

After I share my stories and life, I give the kids time to finish their notes. I make copies of the notes I took for students who were absent or those that couldn't quite keep up. To wrap up, I tell students that we'll use these notes for writing but that we've also learned an important organizational tool they'll be able to use in other subject areas. I ask students to put away their notebooks and tell them we'll be returning to them tomorrow when we begin drafting paragraphs. (Or I may

Figure 1.2 This chart is an example of two-column notes. Notice how they are synthesized from the long version of the story.

MRS. BLAUMAN	
Main idea	**Details**
Story 1, The Dog Lady Mrs. B's time in Alaska—when she first realized she loved dogs!	Lived in Craig, Alaska, after college when she got married Little fishing town Worked in a 4-aisle grocery store Stayed light at night until midnight Dogs would wait outside and walk her home—at least 10 dogs When she went on walks, dogs would join in and she'd have a pack

Figure 1.3 Two-column notes capture information that can be used to draft a descriptive or a persuasive piece.

Main idea	Details
Descriptive—family	2 kids
	Carolynn (note spelling), 22, graduated from CSU, lives in Milwaukee, miss her!
	John, 18, senior at Creek, loves to play lacrosse
	3 amigos—Gunner, Allie, and Dakota, golden retrievers, naughty
Interests/passions	Kids
	Teaching
	Working with teachers and students around the country
	Shoes
	Coffee
	Scuba diving, exploring, reading, gardening, traveling, learning
	Loves to watch sports—especially football (UW Huskies are her fave)

ask them to leave their notebooks open on their desks so that I can do a quick walk-around assessment.) Figure 1.4 is an example of student notes.

» USING TECHNOLOGY

Technology is changing faster than I can write this book. And the kids know and use it well. Although students need to be able to use a paper and pencil and practice stamina, technology also allows for support and remediation and great communication with parents. SMART Board notes can easily be copied and distributed to students who need them (or are absent). Also, they can be posted on blogs or other sites for students and parents to view and access.

Pressing Your Advantage

The lesson that would immediately follow is on drafting (day 2 in this lesson cluster). However, as I share about myself, I also encourage my students to start thinking about what they want to share when it's their turn. My goal is to show that the richer the stories, the better the writing will be. The first week of school we draw names and assign jobs, so the kids (and I) know who will be the first president all the way through to who will be the last. Some years I send a note home to parents with the order and the dates; other years I rely on the students to remember and prepare independently. It's a matter of knowing the class. If I do this same lesson in the spring with a

Figure 1.4 These are two-column notes from a student who is working independently.

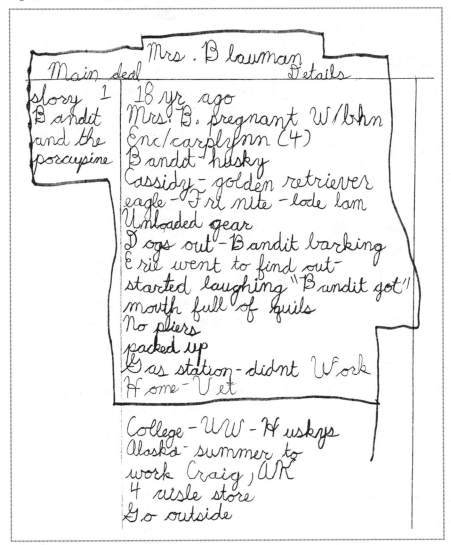

student being interviewed, I still take notes on the document camera, but I write less and expect the students to catch more details.

When the Kids Don't Get It

How about the students who just can't keep up or whose penmanship is illegible or who have learning disabilities that preempt this amount of note taking? That's why I'm scripting—so I can make legible copies for these students. However, I don't give them a pass. After we complete this lesson, I have students leave their notebooks open for me to quickly check/glance at. I confer later (see "One-to-One," below) with the students who seem to be having difficulty.

One-to-One

I notice that Matt isn't keeping up with the notes and is becoming frustrated. I make sure to sit down and confer with him before the day is over so we can come up with a plan for whenever we are taking notes in class. I want him to be successful (and independent).

Me: How was taking notes today?

Matt: It was kind of hard. I couldn't keep up and I missed a lot of stuff.

Me: I could tell that when I saw your notes. How is writing—I mean actual handwriting—for you?

Matt: Hard. And then I can't read it.

Me: So, even if you get it written down, when you go back to read it, it doesn't make sense? I have a couple of options that might help you when we interview our next president. Want to hear them?

Matt: You do? What?

Me: Well, if you're good at typing, I can get you a laptop and you can take notes on that. Or you can handwrite notes from *one* of the stories that are told—because we have to practice handwriting—but then I'll give you a copy of all the notes I'm taking. What do you think?

Matt: I'll try writing. Do I really have to do one whole story?

Me: Yes. Just one. And you have to listen to the rest. Fair?

Matt: Fair.

Owning the Lesson

If you decide that president paragraphs would be a good fit in your room, you need to come prepared with a minimum of two stories and rich details about your life to share with your class. You're modeling what you expect them to do when it's their turn. You're also demonstrating honesty and creating trust. The more students see you as a person, not just a teacher, the stronger sense of community you'll create.

As you read this lesson, did you imagine trying something like it if you haven't already? What aspects do you like? What makes you worry a bit? Notice that the lesson has a dual track—it's about writers discovering topics by revealing their lives *and* it's about learning how to take notes.

Questions to Think About

Think about these questions as you plan your own early-in-the-year writing process lessons:

- How do I establish community?
- How do I share myself and my life outside school with my kids? Do they know me as a person, not just as a teacher?
- Do I feel most comfortable modeling nonfiction writing? Content-area writing? Fiction? Personal narrative?
- How do I want my students to take notes?
- When will they take notes in my classroom and what will they do with these notes?
- How will I have students share information about themselves with their classmates?

Lesson 2

Drafting

Shaping Our Ideas

(day 2 of 5)

Introduction

This lesson shows students how to convert notes into paragraphs. They learn what a paragraph includes and how to construct one. Then they practice drafting their own paragraph.

I tell the kids that we do a couple of types of writing in school. One is "school writing"—you don't see it in the real world but it transfers to authentic writing. Writing single paragraphs usually fits under "school writing," but they need to practice it and they'll have to do it on tests. One of the authors I study a lot, Katie Wood Ray, describes *genres* as the sections of a library or a bookstore—historical fiction, mysteries, biographies, whatever—and calls the writing we do in school one of the *modes* of writing. I teach the kids this distinction as part of my rationale for asking them to write these paragraphs.

The amount of direct instruction I need to provide differs by grade level. Because paragraphing is generally new to third grade, I repeat this lesson until the students are able to write paragraphs independently. I also explicitly deal with what a paragraph is—indenting, a lead (or topic) sentence, detail (supporting) sentences, and then a conclusion—and tell them that a "school" paragraph has to be a *minimum* (and I stress the word) of five complete sentences. By fourth grade, I expect students to know how to construct a paragraph, and there is less direct instruction on this skill. I expect fifth and sixth graders to be able to write well-constructed paragraphs from the get-go.

There are separate "Here's How It Goes" sections for narrative, descriptive (informative/explanatory), and persuasive (opinion) writing. Whatever the type of writing, students use their notes to write a draft paragraph with a lead or topic sentence, details, and a conclusion.

MENTOR TEXTS FOR STUDENTS

NARRATIVE TEXTS

The mentor picture books in lesson 1 are excellent examples of narrative text. A read-aloud novel could also be used. The key is to find narratives that your students enjoy. Some great read-aloud novels are:

- Judy Blume's *Tales of a Fourth Grade Nothing* (Puffin, 1972)
- Kate DiCamillo's *The Tale of Despereaux* (Candlewick, 2003)
- Ingrid Law's *Savvy* (Puffin, 2008)
- Gary Paulsen's *Hatchet* (Simon & Schuster Books for Young Readers, 1987) or *How Angel Peterson Got His Name* (Yearling, 2004)
- Wilson Rawl's *Summer of the Monkeys* (Yearling, 1976)

Third-grade teachers might want to use fables, folktales, and myths as examples of narrative and thus address CCSS RL.3.2. These short, accessible stories reflect diverse cultures.

DESCRIPTIVE (INFORMATIVE/EXPLANATORY) TEXTS

Roald Dahl's stories contain exceptional examples of well-written description. I often read these to the students and let them sketch what they visualize. Three of my favorites are:

- The description of Aunt Sponge and Aunt Spike in *James and the Giant Peach* (Puffin, 1961)
- The description of Mr. Twit in *The Twits* (Puffin, 1980)
- The descriptions (there are several) of the Trunchbull in *Matilda* (Puffin, 1988)

The description of Sistine Bailey in Kate DiCamillo's *The Tiger Rising* (Candlewick, 2001) is another great example.

Jonathan London's informational books also feature good descriptions: *Crocodile: Disappearing Dragon* (Candlewick, 2001), *The Eyes of Gray Wolf* (Chronicle Books, 1993), *Gone Again Ptarmigan* (National Geographic Children's

Books, 2001), *Ice Bear and Little Fox* (Dutton Juvenile, 1998) and *Panther: Shadow of the Swamp* (Candlewick, 2000) are just a few titles. Thomas Locker has great descriptive writing in his informational books as well, especially *Water Dance* (Sandpiper, 1997) and *Cloud Dance* (Sandpiper, 2003).

PERSUASIVE (OPINION) TEXTS

Perhaps the best mentor texts for opinions are in the newspaper—editorials, op-ed pieces, letters to the editor, columns by sports commentators, book reviews—and they can be easily accessed on the Internet and used with the SMART Board.

Mark Teague's books written as letters from Ike LaRue (a dog) are also great examples of persuasive writing. In *Dear Mrs. LaRue, Letters from Obedience School* (Scholastic, 2002), Ike tries to convince his owner to rescue him from obedience "prison"; in *LaRue Across America, Postcards from the Vacation* (The Blue Sky Press, 2011), Ike catalogues the indignities of a road-trip vacation (which was supposed to have been a cruise) with his owner and two cats.

MATERIALS

- Previous day's notes in spiral notebooks (students)
- Pencils (students and teacher)
- Highlighter (students and teacher)
- Mentor text(s) (or any writing guide that shows examples of the appropriate types of paragraphs and defines them) and some means of displaying them (teacher)

TIME: 60 minutes

▶ THE NITTY-GRITTY

This circles back to the reality that faces educators. We must teach students how to construct paragraphs that can be assessed on tests.

Here's How It Goes (Narrative Paragraphs)

"Three types of school writing are narrative, descriptive, and persuasive. But lots of these types of writing are also done outside school. So what we're going to learn will get you ready for school and for writing in real life."

"Of course you don't walk into Barnes and Noble and ask for the descriptive section—they'd think you were crazy. But I need to teach you how to write a descriptive paragraph—that's an educational standard. I also need to teach you how to write a narrative paragraph and that's what we're going to work on today.

A narrative paragraph tells a story and often answers the questions *Who? What? When? Where? Why?* and *How?* Follow along as I read an example."

> They were all waiting for him. Waiting. Sistine was waiting, too; waiting for him to do something. He looked down at the ground and saw what they had thrown at her. It was an apple. He stared at it for what seemed like a long time, and when he looked back up, they were all waiting to see what he would do.
>
> And so he ran. After a minute, he could tell they were running after him; he didn't need to look back to see if they were there. He knew it. He knew the feeling of being chased. He dropped the picture of the tiger and ran full out, pumping his legs and arms hard. They were still behind him. A sudden thrill went through him when he realized that what he was doing was saving Sistine Bailey.

"Notice how these two paragraphs home in on a specific event, showing action and allowing us to visualize what's happening. They use strong verbs. This is what I want you to do in your own writing." Most of the students agree that these paragraphs retell a story and are game for writing one of their own.

▶ THE NITTY-GRITTY

Finding a *single* narrative paragraph in a piece of literature is tough to do. But there are many examples of *consecutive* narrative paragraphs. This example is from Kate DiCamillo's *The Tiger Rising* (2001).

I then put the notes from the previous day up on the board. "Okay, now you've seen how a narrative looks. You noticed that the author followed a sequence—the story was written in the order it happened. Today you're going to work on a rough draft of a paragraph about me. I say rough draft because tomorrow we may change it. In the writing process, authors need time to plan or rehearse or think about what they're going to write. You will be writing—retelling, really—one of the stories about me. But because we only took short notes, you're going to have to add a lot. The notes we took yesterday were our prewriting. Let's get them out.

"I told a lot of stories yesterday, but you only have to write one. Why don't you look through your notes and see which one jumps out at you." I give kids time to do this.

"Now I want you to take a highlighter and put a box around the section you want to write about. For example, if I wanted to write about Bandit and the porcupine, I'd box this whole section." As I explain, I model what I want the kids to do by boxing a section in the notes.

▶ **THE NITTY-GRITTY**

Highlighting and boxing the information helps focus the student and limits the extraneous information. Notice too that students get to *choose* which story they want to write.

Starting out. "Before I have you write, I'm going to model the process for you. I know a paragraph has to indent, so I'm going to do that. Even though this is a rough draft, I want to practice correctly so it becomes a good habit. Next I have to come up with a lead sentence, or a 'grabber.' Some teachers call them *topic sentences*. The main thing is that the first sentence has to catch the reader's attention and introduce what the paragraph is about. Sometimes a question can do that. For example, I could write, *Has your dog ever tried to eat a porcupine? Well, my teacher's dog did and here's the story*. Or I could start with what I remember most about the story. For example, *My teacher loves her dogs, but she wasn't too happy the time Bandit, her husky, ruined the family camping trip by trying to eat a porcupine*. What else could you come up with?" We generate ideas and I jot them down, so all students have a lead to hold on to.

Graphic organizer. I introduce a simple graphic organizer (Figure 1.5) that reminds students to indent paragraphs. I call this organizer *Utah Flipped* (if you pull out a map of the United States and rotate Utah ninety degrees counterclockwise, you end up with this outline), and it remains up in the room for students to refer to. "I'm showing you this to remind you that you need to indent your paragraph. What I want you to do now is write your lead sentence. Then I want

Figure 1.5 The "Utah Flipped" Graphic Organizer

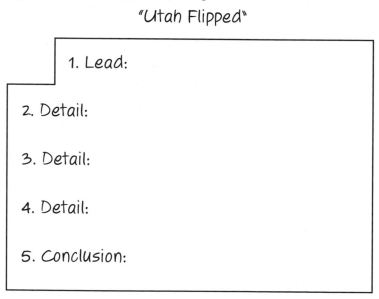

"Utah Flipped"

1. Lead:

2. Detail:

3. Detail:

4. Detail:

5. Conclusion:

you to look at your notes—remembering that order or sequence is important to narrative—and start writing."

Invariably, a student will raise a hand and ask, "How long does this have to be? How many sentences?" My response? "Generally, paragraphs are all different lengths. The main thing is that you write well and get your point across with enough information so that your reader understands your intent without getting bored. If you want a simple answer, a 'school' paragraph has to be a *minimum* of five sentences—but that's a minimum. Remember, this is a first draft, so we get to go back and make it better. I want to see how you guys do. I'll be walking around the room and conferring with you as you work."

Now I turn the kids loose to write. I move around the room and confer, nudging students to add more and checking on sequencing. I am informally assessing how the students approach this task. Are they comfortable getting right to work with the writing? Do they seem to need me? Who can't get to work? Who

▶ **THE NITTY-GRITTY**

That's *my* answer in *my* classroom. What are your expectations? What do the students need to do in your classroom? Right from the beginning, be explicit about expectations for your students.

CCSS, *GRADE BY GRADE*

Third-grade teachers, your students should be developing a paragraph about a real event using effective technique, descriptive details, and clear event sequences and providing a sense of closure. Basically your students need to learn how to construct a paragraph that centers on one main idea, includes strong sequential details, and finishes with a strong ending.

Fourth-grade teachers, your students should also be developing a paragraph about a real event using effective technique, descriptive details, and clear event sequences, but they should also use a variety of transitional words and phrases to manage the sequence of events and then provide a conclusion that follows from the narrated experiences or events. You see how this builds on what third graders are expected to do. Writing becomes more sophisticated and detailed, and students learn to use a variety of transitional words (without, you hope, being formulaic) and finishing strong.

Fifth-grade teachers, your students should also be developing a paragraph about a real event using effective technique, descriptive details, and clear event sequences but also using a variety of transitional words, phrases, *and clauses* to manage the sequence of events and then providing a conclusion that follows from the narrated experience or events.

Sixth-grade teachers, you make a big jump. Instead of single paragraphs, your students are required to write entire pieces (for example, "Write informative/explanatory texts to examine a topic and convey ideas, concepts, and information through the selection, organization, and analysis of relevant content"). Introductions, details, and conclusions are required, but paragraphs are still the essential ingredients.

plunges right in? Who is satisfied with the bare minimum and doesn't know what to do after that? This information helps me during writing workshop.

I generally allow thirty minutes for the students to complete their rough drafts of the paragraphs. As we all know, though, students don't all finish writing at the same time, so those who finish early may move on to something else (like reading), and those who want to write more may finish later if needed.

▶ THE NITTY-GRITTY

I steer the students away from writing about my family, as this doesn't truly describe me and often turns into a list. Although it's great to learn about our classmate's families, they're probably not the best fodder for descriptive writing. When I read descriptive paragraphs that are listlike or without any main idea, I know I need to do some direct teaching, whether in a small group or one-to-one.

Here's How It Goes: Descriptive/ Informative/Explanatory Paragraphs

Writing a descriptive paragraph tends to be a bit more difficult than a narrative one, because students have to choose from a lot of information and then create a topic sentence and stick to one main idea. I model these paragraphs much more often than I do narrative paragraphs. I'm always looking for great examples— from students but also from descriptive writing in novels and other texts. This is the perfect time to read excerpts from Roald Dahl in which he captures the idiosyncrasies of his characters and allow the students to sketch and use his words to help them visualize. I also urge students to highlight sections of their drafts in which they have written an especially descriptive sentence. Figurative language is a powerful tool for creating great descriptive writing.

"Last week we talked about types of writing—school writing and authentic, real-world writing. Today we're going to look at descriptive writing. I think you already know that good writers write with awesome description—they help the reader visualize and create sensory images.

"Let's get our president notebooks out again and look at the sections that describe me. If you just write about my family is that really describing me? Probably not. How could you describe me so that if a new student passed me in the hall they might know that it's me? Take out your highlighters again and highlight in your notes what you'd like to include in this paragraph.

"I think coming up with a lead sentence or topic sentence in a descriptive paragraph is a little tougher than coming up with one for a narrative. Remember, the lead sentence needs to capture the *main idea* of the paragraph—and all the rest of the sentences need to support it. So if you write *Mrs. Blauman has two children that she really loves*, then the rest of the paragraph needs to be about Carolynn and John. And that doesn't really describe me. Can you guys come up with some leads and I'll write them down?" Students brainstorm possible leads.

Here's How It Goes: Persuasive/Opinion Paragraphs

Before we even begin to write persuasive paragraphs, we have a class discussion of all the ways we use persuasion in our lives, not just in writing.

"Have you ever tried to talk your parents into allowing you to go to a party or a friend's house even after they've said no?" Lots of agreement from the students. "Think of all the times you've had an opinion or tried to convince someone of something—you usually do it by talking. But often we attempt to persuade others in writing as well. Authors do it all the time when they create empathy in the reader— they're persuading you to feel a certain way about a character. Think about characters you've loved and those you've disliked. You've felt that way because the author has written persuasively. Let's take a few minutes and just brainstorm all the ways you've used persuasion in your life. Jot a quick list in your president notebook." Students quickly get to work. Figure 1.6 is a page from Jake's notebook. He's gone a step further and indicated whether he was successful or not.

After students share, we create a class anchor chart of all the ways we have seen persuasive or opinion writing in real life (see Figure 1.7).

"There are lots of ways to write persuasive pieces, but I'm going to have you write a generic letter of recommendation for our president. Usually letters of recommendation are for a job, but I want you to write about why he is special or an outstanding member of our class. You know a lot about him and what makes him unique, so I want you to think of three examples of why he is a special young man. Jot those down." We brainstorm examples as a class.

"I'm going to pass out an example of a letter of recommendation (Figure 1.8). Please read it through. I want you to leave tracks in the snow about how you notice it's organized."

After students have read the letter, we discuss its structure: It has an introduction stating Sally's three main strengths, it has a short paragraph describing each of those strengths, and then it has a concluding paragraph reiterating why Sally is special. With this formula to help them, the kids are ready to have a go.

Press Your Advantage

What does this lesson look like later in the year? Students are now writing paragraphs independently but incorporating skills we are learning in class. For example, if we are studying similes, I expect students to add a simile to their writing. If we are working on strong verbs, I require that students use more active verbs than passive verbs in their paragraphs. I use these paragraphs to practice and reinforce the specific writing skills my grade-level curriculum requires that I teach!

Figure 1.6 Jake's List

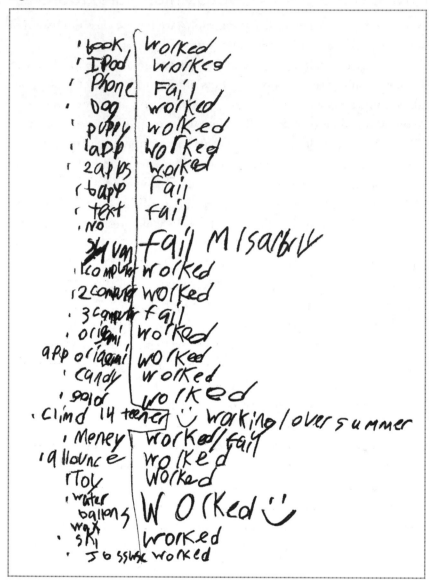

When the Kids Don't Get It

As students are writing their drafts and I move around the room, I identify the students who are struggling and need direct instruction then and there. If I have a handful of students who need more support, I gather them in a group and we write a draft together, using an even more detailed organizer and dropping information from our notes into it. After filling in the organizer, all that's left is for them to write it out individually.

Figure 1.7 Class Anchor Chart: Real-Life Persuasive Writing

Newspaper–sports section, commentary, editorials, ads	Twitter
Movie ads	Sign twirlers (human arrows)
Commercials	Beggars
Billboards	Special offers
Previews	Paid programs
Bumper stickers	Mailers (junk mail)
Labels	Email ads
Blurbs on books	Street vendors
YouTube	Radio
Samples	Talk shows
Business flyers	"Teasers" on TV
Pop-up ads	Coupons
Invitations	Debates
Book reviews	Political ads
Court cases (briefs)	Political yard signs
Airplane banners	Résumés
Blogs, ads, etc. on the Internet	Letters of recommendation

One-to-One

While the other students get right to work, Essence sits listlessly looking at her open notebook. When I checked her notes the previous day, she had done well, but now she appears to be at a loss. I sit down beside her.

▶ **THE NITTY-GRITTY**

There are tons of graphic organizers available—blackline masters you can copy and those you can pull up on a computer. Thinking Maps, eight visual teaching tools developed by Dr. David Hyerle, are another great way for kids to organize. Choose what works for *the student*. The Utah Flipped organizer works for me—especially with my learning disabled students.

Figure 1.8 Example Letter of Recommendation

April 20, 2011

To Whom It May Concern,

I have been fortunate to have been a student with Sally Silvershoes for the past year at P.S. 110. I am pleased to recommend her based on what I know about her. Sally is a quiet and responsible student, a good friend to others, and has interests outside school.

Everyone in class wants to sit next to Sally because she focuses on her work and doesn't interfere with others. She is also helpful to others. If you have a question or don't understand, she always helps. That's because she listens to the teacher and pays attention. I think she would bring this same responsibility to anything she does.

Sally is also a good friend. When kids at school get into fights, she sticks up for anyone being bullied. But she doesn't get in the middle of things or tattle. Sally will go get adult help if it's needed. She's also really good at listening and helping friends who are sad. Sally is good at making others feel better. She's also good at getting friends who are fighting to talk to each other and work things out.

Finally, while Sally is good at school, she also has other interests. She loves soccer and has been playing since she was four years old. That shows that she's really committed to it and is a hard worker. She loves soccer and loves to play on a team.

These are just a few things about Sally that make her a special person. They show that she is responsible, kind and a hard worker. I highly recommend her.

Sincerely,

Alex Masters

Me: Which story do you want to write about? Maybe the one you know the most about?

Essence: I remember the first story you told best. About when you were in Alaska. I just don't know how to write it.

Me: Okay, let's take one of these Utah Flipped graphs. See how it has space for five sentences? Let's find five things in your notes about Alaska. We're going to start with five, but as we continue to do these and practice, you're going to add more. How do you want to start?

Essence: "Mrs. B. lived in Alaska."

Me: Yes, that's the main idea, but do you think it grabs the reader? Why did I tell you this story?

Essence: Oh, 'cause that's when you fell in love with dogs and they called you the Dog Lady.

Me: Right. Think of some of the examples the kids were giving about possible lead sentences. Did you like any of those?

Essence: I could write, "Have you ever had a teacher called the Dog Lady? Mine was when she lived in Alaska." [*Even though that's two sentences, it works beautifully as a lead!*]

Me: That would work. See how I put that by number 1—your lead? [*I'm scripting for Essence, as writing is tough for her.*] Because that tells the main idea. Now the rest of the paragraph needs to be about me in Alaska and dogs. Can you look at your notes and see what would make sense to write next? We need to add details.

Essence: That you worked in a four-aisle store and the dogs would wait for you?

Leslie: That works. Tell me how you want the sentence to read and I'll write it down.

Essence: "Mrs. B. worked in a four-aisle store and the dogs would wait outside for her." Can I write for sentence three that they would walk you home?

Me: Absolutely [*I'm scribing*]. What other detail do you want?

Essence: "When she took walks the dogs always followed and it was like a pack."

Me: Terrific. Now, we have to end this so that your reader knows that you're done. I've found that sometimes it helps to *lift*, or use a word from your first sentence in your last sentence. Is there something there that you could repeat?

▶ **THE NITTY-GRITTY**

Students who struggle with writing benefit from telling the story out loud first. Doing so solidifies and organizes thoughts, making the writing a bit easier. At the beginning of the year I will scribe or script for my students who struggle, gradually turning this responsibility over to them.

Essence: Maybe "Dog Lady"?

Me: What do you want to say about that?

Essence: "Since there were always so many dogs around her, the people in town started calling Mrs. B. the Dog Lady."

Me: Anything else?

Essence: No. I think that's enough.

Me: Okay, now it's your turn to take the notes off this planner and rewrite it as a paragraph. [*While the paragraph is minimal, this is a start. We will continue to elaborate and Essence will need more direct instruction.*]

Owning the Lesson

We need to give kids ample background knowledge before they write. Writing is messy, and from experience—both as writers and teachers—we all come at it from different directions. How can we support our students and get them writing right from the start? How can we make their first attempts at drafting positive ones, so they will want to return to the writing? Although writing is hard, how can we make writing workshop one of the highlights of the day?

This section includes options for narrative, descriptive (informative/ explanatory), and persuasive (opinion) paragraphs. What do your students need? How do you scaffold this type of writing in your classroom so that it transfers into all the content areas? Do you have to do all the types of paragraphs each week or could you spread this out over the year?

Questions to Think About

- What type of text do I want to teach my students?
- How do I want students to create their drafts? Do I want them to handwrite them or use a word processor?
- How can I scaffold writing/drafting for my students?
- How do I ensure that it's a positive experience?
- How do I provide feedback to my students? Where am I while my students are drafting?
- Do I have to start with narrative? What about descriptive or persuasive writing?

Revising

Looking at Our Work with New Eyes

(day 3 of 5)

Introduction

In this lesson students revise their rough drafts by improving content and language. Revision ("vision again") is looking at writing with new eyes. I find this is the toughest part of the process for kids. When I ask them what *revision* is, they immediately answer by listing editing skills—that's the way they perceive making the writing better. I address (and change) this skewed understanding directly. As writers we don't revise everything we do. However, when we publish our work or present it to an audience, we need to revise. If it's worth the effort of finalizing, it's worth the effort of revising. As an example, I bring in the reams of papers I've printed as I've revised this book. I bring in all the sticky notes and comments from my "wise eyes"—the folks who have read and commented on my writing.

> **CCSS, GRADE BY GRADE**
>
> Third-grade teachers, your students should focus on temporal words and phrases to signal event order. Fourth- and fifth-grade teachers, your students should use concrete words and phrases and sensory details to convey experiences and events precisely. In these descriptors, language and specific words are the road to revision. Lesson Clusters Two and Three include specific lessons on how to increase vocabulary and add figurative language.

MENTOR TEXTS FOR TEACHERS

Barry Lane has written many professional books on revision, among them *After the End* (1993). His *Reviser's Toolbox* (1999) is filled with blackline masters and writing exercises that are perfect for writing workshop. His analogy to the way binoculars make a view clearer and more focused—"zooming in" on writing—is concrete for all grade levels. I have a pair of binoculars hanging on our writing board (along with a magnifying glass) to remind students to look closely at the world.

MENTOR TEXTS FOR STUDENTS

Returning to the mentor texts from lessons 1 and 2 and revisiting how the authors helped the reader visualize is key to this lesson. Examples of mentor texts for word play are any of the *Fancy Nancy* books, by Jane O'Connor and Robin Preiss Glasser. *Fancy Nancy's Favorite Fancy Words from Accessories to Zany* (Harper-Collins, 2008) encourages students to consult a thesaurus for other word choices. A great book for descriptive writing and incorporating similes is Hanoch Piven's *My Dog Is as Smelly as Dirty Socks* (Random House, 2007).

MATERIALS

- President notebooks (students)
- Rough drafts (students)
- Gel pens (students and teacher)

TIME: 45 minutes

▶ **THE NITTY-GRITTY**

I got the gel pen idea from a colleague, Mark Overmeyer, in his book *When Writer's Workshop Isn't Working* (2005). The novelty of a new writing implement gets the kids excited. The pens are also a concrete way to delineate the difference between *revision* and editing. In our classroom, gel pens are used only for revision. And I keep the pens in a real toolbox!

Here's How It Goes

After explicitly discussing what revision is, I continue, "You all know I love to write, but sometimes it's incredibly hard—and sometimes it's scary to share your writing with others. Especially if you're worried that they're going to tear your writing apart. That happened to me in college. I was taking an upper-level writing class, and I loved the teacher, but one of the requirements was that we had to meet outside class with a writing group and share and discuss one another's writing. Our teacher put the groups together, and I was with a bunch of people I didn't know. And they thought it made them look smarter if they told you all the things you did wrong in your writing—basically they hammered you. I shared one of my pieces and they shredded it. I was incredibly embarrassed. So the next week when we met, I 'forgot' my writing. Did I really forget it?"

Naomi pipes up, "No. I wouldn't take my writing either. That was really mean of them."

"Yes, it was. And it didn't help me as a writer. Would you believe that for the rest of that trimester I didn't share again? That's kind of sad. If it were me now I would say something, but back then I was too embarrassed. I tell that story because in here we are going to share a lot with one another—and we're going to ask a lot of questions—but we're going to ask questions that help make the writing clearer. And we're going to tell one another all the great things we're doing in our writing. We all have to feel safe.

"So today you're going to share your paragraph with a partner. As you read your draft, your partner is going to tell you what she or he likes and also ask questions. That is your purpose—not just to say, *That's really good*, but to help your partner improve the piece.

"Your job as the author is to change some of your writing and possibly to add to it. Then you'll switch and you'll help your partner write even better. But here's the best part. When we revise we get to use the gel pens—that way as your writing teacher when I see gel pen ink on a paper I know that you've been revising."

THE LANGUAGE OF LEARNING

Share yourself as a writer! Writing is hard and scary and many teachers don't like to teach it. Share your stories and your trials and tribulations. If the kids view you as a writer who struggles with writing at times, they will be more willing to take risks.

TO LEARN MORE

For more on teaching students how to talk, see the Phenomenal Talk lesson in Chapter 3 of my book *The Inside Guide to The Reading–Writing Classroom: Strategies for Extraordinary Teaching*.

THE LANGUAGE OF LEARNING

You must be explicit about your purpose. Merely sending the kids off to talk about their writing won't help them improve. Giving them a bit of time to reflect afterward is also beneficial. Posing a simple *How'd it go?* or *Tell me one thing you did to improve your piece after your conference* when they've finished holds them accountable. I often have the kids think about these questions and write their answers on the back of their rough draft. I sometimes ask them to write one *specific* way their partner helped them improve their writing, or to go back and highlight (in gel pen) a place they revised and then explain *why* that helps the piece. Here are some specific ways to prompt your students to revise their work:

- Where do you think your reader might get confused? How can you add details to help them understand?

- Does your piece go in order or does it jump around? Can you move sections to make it clearer?
- Have you helped your reader visualize or create sensory images? Highlight where. If you haven't done this, can you add descriptive details?
- Highlight where you've used figurative language (simile, metaphor, personification, etc.). If you don't have anything highlighted, add figurative language.
- Highlight your action words in one color and all the other verbs in another color. Do you have more action verbs? If not, add some!
- Highlight the first word in every sentence. What do you notice? Does each sentence start with a different word?
- Highlight your transitions. Do they make sense?
- Does your lead or topic sentence grab the reader?
- Does your conclusion let your reader know you're done?
- Have you added details and facts to convince your reader?

Remember to keep it simple—have them choose one or two at a time (no more), or you'll overwhelm them. It's all about purpose!

With that, my students set off with their partners to revise their pieces. I generally allow twenty minutes for this activity—ten for each student. After ten minutes I tell the students to switch roles.

Press Your Advantage

I collect the rough drafts, read them, and write my own revision comments. I do this when I can focus my attention on each child's writing without being distracted. My revision comments primarily point out what the student is doing well, but I may include a few nudges to *add more* (I also explain why that will help). Our words as teachers—spoken and written—are powerful, and my comments to my students are *positive*. I want to highlight their *strengths*; what they are doing well. (I can do the teaching/fix-ups in individual conferences.) I have two guiding principles:

- Because this is *revision*, I am very careful not to make any *editing* marks on their papers. I don't want to confuse the students about these two different processes.

- Even though I'm not editing the students' papers, I still take editing notes for myself so I can work on specific skills with specific students. If I notice specific weaknesses that appear to be widespread, those skills will be editing minilessons I present to the entire class.

When the Kids Don't Get It

As I read through the revised paragraphs, I look specifically for examples at both ends of the spectrum.

Of course I look for exemplary work in which students have added detail to their pieces. (The gel pens make it easy to recognize the changes students have made. Also, the kids *love* the gel pens, and knowing they are *only* for revision helps them focus on doing it well.) I put these papers on the document camera and discuss them, showing the students what I expect. I only use papers that are positive, and I ask students for permission first. I also take their names off the papers so there is no embarrassment.

But I look as well for the students who have done little or no revision. If there are quite a few of them, I pull them together to work on revision as a group. If there are just one or two kids, I confer with them individually.

▶ **THE NITTY-GRITTY**

A copy of the record chart I use to take my editing notes is included in Appendix A. Appendix B is an overview of the year that shows the types of revision lessons I teach when. For example, in the early fall I'm working on organization (especially topic sentences and conclusions) and word choice. By late fall, my focus moves to figurative language, verbs, and sentence length. Check out what we focus on as the year progresses!

THE LANGUAGE OF LEARNING

As I work with teachers around the country, the following revision metaphor seems to stick. It's easy to understand and a great visual reminder for adding details. A paragraph that has main ideas but no details is like a tree with a few branches but no leaves. The details are the leaves. Each branch needs at least one leaf. Kids can draw three posters—a bare-branched tree, a tree with a few blossoms, and a tree covered with leaves. As writers, what should we strive for? Adding details, of course—as long as they improve the writing. (Sometimes more doesn't mean better.)

One-to-One

After reading and responding to each student's rough draft, I note that Frank has only changed one word; he's on my conference radar screen. My goal is to find out his thoughts about and process for revision and then teach him how to add details so that the reader can visualize. It's always about *purpose*.

Me: How'd it go yesterday with revision? Can you tell me a little about what you decided to do to make your piece better? [*Frank's notebook, open to his rough draft, is on his desk*.]

Frank: I added this word right here.

Me: Okay, tell me why you did that.

Frank: Because you said we had to add something so I decided to add that Bandit barked *loud*.

Me: So you started to add detail. I'm going to read what you've written and I want you to think about the story I told. If you hadn't heard me tell the story and you were just listening to this, do you think you'd understand about Bandit trying to eat the porcupine? [*I read Frank's paragraph out loud and then pause while he thinks.*]

Frank: I didn't tell everything.

Me: And you don't have to, but let's go back to your notes and see if there are some things that you might want to add. That's the coolest part of writing—that we can continue to change it and make it better. To help your reader picture it. What do you remember most?

Frank [*after going back through his notes and pointing to two details*]: I could add that you guys had to pack everything back up and go home, and I could add the part about trying to get the quills out with the pliers. That was funny.

Me: Why was it funny?

Frank: Because you were pregnant and lying on top of Bandit to hold him down and you still couldn't get the quills out.

Me: That's it! You could see it—visualize it—and that's exactly what you want to do for your reader. Show me where in your draft you'd add those details so that it would make sense.

Frank: Right here. But how do I fit them in?

Me: You could take the gel pen and draw an arrow out to the margin and add it, or you could put an asterisk to mark that you want to add it—like a key—and then put another asterisk at the bottom of the page and write what you want to add. Authors use that trick all the time. Want to try it? [*Frank nods and gets to work.*]

Owning the Lesson

Even after almost thirty years of teaching—at a variety of grade levels—I still find that revision is the toughest part of the writing process for kids to tackle. It's hard to change your writing. It's even harder to change your writing when it's something you don't care about. Revision should be saved for only those pieces that are going to make it to final publication. Not all writing is revised. I've also found that when students have a focus or purpose for their revision, it's easier and more manageable. Although it is powerful for students to own their revision, it also helps immensely if they get feedback from their peers and their teacher.

How often do you want your students to take pieces all the way through the writing process? How often do you want them to revise, and what specifically are your goals? Think about yourself as a writer and how you feel about revision. How can you bring this background into the classroom? If you're using the president paragraphs in your classroom, how can you build in time for revision? Are you going to read all the papers also, or will you eventually turn that responsibility over to the students?

Questions to Think About

- How often do I want students to revise?

- Do students revise on their own? With partners? In a group? With me?

- Do students know how to talk and to ask one another questions to drive revision and clarity?

- Do students feel safe enough to share their thinking with their peers?

- Do I have specific things that I want them to do (e.g., action verbs, strong nouns, figurative language)?

- Do they add or cut from their paper? Do they know how?

- Do students know how to revise using a word processor?

- Is there an author's chair or some other avenue for students to read their work to the entire class and receive feedback?

THE LANGUAGE OF LEARNING

In many writing classrooms, time is set aside at the beginning or end of writing workshop for students to share their writing with the entire class and ask for feedback. Sometimes students sign up to share, other times the teacher may invite them to share, especially after a writing conference. Students generally sit in the author's chair (in my classroom they sit in my director's chair and I sit on the floor with the class).

I ask each author what he or she would like help with, what we should focus on. He or she answers and begins to read. A caution—*limit the length!* I only allow students to read one or two pages—maximum—so we can focus on the writing. When the author finishes, the class and I give positive feedback. I generally go first at the beginning of the year, and I'm always specific. Instead of "I really liked that," I'll say, "Your line [I quote it] with the simile in it really helped me visualize what was happening." After other students have shared their responses, we discuss the author's specific request for help or focus. We might ask questions or point out where we were confused, but always in a way that moves the writing forward. Ultimately, the author gets to decide whether or not to use our advice! (Remember, modeling is incredibly important for this to be successful!)

Editing

Polishing Our Writing

(day 4 of 5)

Introduction

This lesson focuses on using correct grammar and mechanics for your students' grade level. At the beginning of the year, many of my students think this is the most important part of writing. Maybe that's because they're tested on it so often. I want my students to use grammar and conventions correctly *in their writing*, not in isolation.

We are judged on the appearance of the text and the quality of our proofreading before the reader gets to the content. I tell my students that no matter how terrific the content, if readers can't get past misspelled words and poor grammar, they're never going to be able to enjoy the writing. I also tell them that *once you know the rules*, editing becomes easier. You are the one in charge of the content, but the editing rules remain the same. An editor or computer can help you edit, but they can't do the writing. The hardest part of writing is the content. Editing is the finishing touch—applying the polish. If we are displaying our work for the public, it needs to shine. I reassure my students that this year I will help them be their own editor.

Editing is a large component of the CCSS. Students need to be able to edit both in isolation and in an authentic context. In my classroom, we edit authentically. To determine which editing skills to focus on at the beginning of the year, I look at the benchmarks for the previous year. For example, if I'm teaching fourth grade, what are the grammar and mechanics skills that all third graders were expected to master? Those are my editing "nonnegotiables" at the beginning of the year.

CCSS, *GRADE BY GRADE*

Some specifics from Conventions of Standard English, Standard 2:

• Third graders should capitalize appropriate words in titles, form and use possessives, use conventional spelling for high-frequency words, and consult reference materials to check and correct spellings.

• Fourth graders should use correct capitalization and spell grade-appropriate words correctly, consulting references as needed.

• Fifth graders should use most punctuation correctly and spell grade-appropriate words correctly, consulting references as needed.

• Sixth graders should demonstrate a command of the conventions of standard English capitalization, punctuation, and spelling and also use punctuation (commas, parentheses, dashes) to set off nonrestrictive/parenthetical elements in increasingly sophisticated writing. Sixth graders are expected to spell correctly.

MENTOR TEXT FOR STUDENTS

- Robin Pulver's *Punctuation Takes a Vacation* (Holiday House, 2003)

MENTOR TEXT FOR TEACHERS

- Lynne Truss' *Eats, Shoots, and Leaves* (2006)

MATERIALS

- Rough drafts (students)
- Pens (students)
- Dictionaries (students)

TIME: 30 minutes

▶ **THE NITTY-GRITTY**

I have my students use print dictionaries at first, so they become familiar with how dictionaries are organized (being able to use a printed dictionary is also a Common Core Standard). Computers are great, but they preclude the need to learn and practice certain basic skills.

Here's How It Goes

I return the rough drafts with my written comments about revision and ask students to spend five minutes or so addressing my "nudges" by adding to or clarifying their writing. After that we regroup and I ask them what editing is. After a short discussion, I sum up.

"Yes, editing is important—and it's usually what gets noticed first by the reader. But remember, once you know how to edit well, you're set. If later in life you're writing a book or an article for publication, your editors and proofreaders will catch mistakes. I'm going to be your editor for a while this year, but I want you to be able to find and correct as many mistakes as you can yourselves. Would you believe that our ears catch mistakes better than our eyes? So when you're editing your piece, I'd like you to read it out loud. You may have noticed that when I'm checking over something I've written, I read it softly to myself. That's because I trust my ears. So I want you to do that and fix the mistakes you can. Correct the spelling words that are our nonnegotiables.

"But here's the deal. I want you trying amazing, great vocabulary, and if I made you look up all those tough words in the dictionary, you'd never attempt them, right? Take a look through your piece and see if you've used some tough words. Who's got one?"

Conor raises his hand. "*Phenomenal*."

"Awesome! Circle it and I'll spell it for you. And you also know that you're not allowed to follow me around and ask me how to spell words. If you circle the words that you think are misspelled, I'll write the correct spelling when I'm doing the editing for you. However, if I find a misspelled word, I'll circle it and you'll have to look it up in the dictionary. What do you think? Fair?"

"I think I'd rather have you do the work," Dexter says—and he's right. But he's also doing the work by *identifying* the words he's misspelled in his draft.

Students independently edit their pieces, this time in pen (regular, not gel), and then exchange papers with a peer for one more go-round. Then they turn them in, and I edit them that evening. (And I hold the kids to my misspelled-words expectations.) I also note which students need guided instruction on specific editing skills (Which students still are unable to construct complete sentences? Who needs punctuation practice?). Later I provide small-group direct instruction for these students.

Pressing Your Advantage

Students receive their edited papers back the following day, and the dictionaries come out! Students who didn't find their misspelled words have to look them up—a hard lesson, but they learn quickly.

> ▶ **THE NITTY-GRITTY**
>
> My kids know the non-negotiables because we have a poster displaying the grade-level "no excuse" (high-frequency) spelling words and have discussed the editing that is a must. (For example, all third, fourth, and fifth graders need to start sentences with a capital and end with some form of punctuation. The word *I* is always capitalized.) We add to our nonnegotiables as new skills are taught throughout the year.

As we continue to practice editing, I introduce checklists that the students turn in with their work before I edit it. These checklists itemize the grammar and mechanics that I expect students to use independently and that I hold them accountable for. (See the example in Figure 1.9.)

My ultimate goal is for students to find errors themselves. So I eventually stop circling errors and instead put an asterisk (*) in the margin of their draft to indicate that there is an error on a specific line. (One asterisk means one error, two asterisks on the same line indicate two errors, etc.) It's up to the student to find the error(s). I also suggest that parents use this strategy, so that the kids do their own editing at home as well. However, I continue to work with my students who need a great deal of support.

When the Kids Don't Get It

I ask kids who have no sense of editing, who don't know where to start, to join my editing group. Each time I work with them, we focus on just *one thing*. Perhaps our first lesson is using capitals and periods to mark the beginning or ending of a sentence, or spelling basic words—whatever these kids need *most* right now. After each group meeting, I expect them to use that skill correctly from that point forward, even though I still correct the rest of their piece.

To Learn More

For further information on how to incorporate an editing timeline into your year, see Appendix A.

One-to-One

Oscar raises his hand and tells me he is done with his editing, so I stop beside his desk. I noticed his lack of editing last night when I read his draft, so I'm curious about what he's accomplished today. He has quite a few details in his writing, he stays on topic, his voice comes through, but there are no capitals and periods. I need to teach these skills.

Me: How did editing go?

Oscar: Okay. See, I circled a couple words I didn't know how to spell.

Me: I see that. But as your writing teacher, I also notice something else. You have a capital letter at the beginning of your paragraph and a period at the end of the paragraph, but nowhere else. Why do we use capitals and periods?

Oscar: To show sentences?

Figure 1.9 Editing Checklist

Name _____ Title of Piece _____

	I did this in my piece	I didn't do this in my piece and need to fix it	The author did it	The author didn't do it
Area	**Self**	**Self**	**Partner**	**Partner**
Spelling				
Correct the words I know				
Circle the words I don't know				
Capitals				
Beginning word of the sentence				
People's names				
Other proper nouns				
Punctuation				
Endmarks				
Commas				
Other				

COMMENTS:

Partner's name _____

Me: Right. So when I read this, I see just one huge sentence. I'm going to read it to you. [*I read the entire paragraph out loud in one breath*.] What do you think?

Oscar [*laughing*]: That you couldn't breathe.

Me: When I do that, do you see how important capitals and periods are? And as writers we need to get in the habit of adding them even as we're drafting. Now what I want you to do with me is read this out loud. And when you think you need to take a breath or pause, I want you to stop. [*Oscar begins to read and stops at the point where his sentence should end*.]

Me: Perfect. You stopped at the end of your thought. What do you need to put there to show the reader to end?

Oscar: A period. [*He adds it to his paper*.]

Me: Great. Now what do you need to do to show the next word starts a sentence?

Oscar: Put a capital. [*He does that, and we continue to edit the rest of his paragraph the same way*.]

Me: Okay, you did the end all by yourself. From this point forward, do I expect you to use capitals and periods? Is it okay if I see you reading it out loud to yourself so that your ears will help you?

Oscar: Yes. I'll try.

And I hold him accountable. Oscar needs to take this lesson to heart and then use the skill independently.

Owning the Lesson

Grammar and mechanics can look so different depending on the context. As teachers we often give our students practice sentences to get them ready for test-type editing questions. But this doesn't always transfer to authentic editing: finding and correcting our own mistakes. We need to give kids lots of help with this. Think about it—even if you write an amazing résumé and the content is beyond reproach, if it's riddled with spelling and grammatical errors, you'll never make it to the interview. Editing is only one part of the writing process, but it's a large part of how we are judged. Let's teach our children how to do it well. Once they have this skill, they've got it for life!

How do you teach grammar and mechanics in your room? And how does that transfer into authentic writing? How could you use the president paragraphs to incorporate editing skills into the writer's workshop? If your students spend part of one writer's workshop a week focusing on editing skills, how will that improve their writing?

Questions to Think About

- How often do I have students edit their own work versus complete editing worksheets?
- How do I hold my students accountable for editing correctly?
- What about students who need more time and practice?
- What about students who need to be enriched?
- How are grammar and mechanics skills taught in my classroom?

Finalizing

Taking Our Work Public

(day 5 of 5)

Introduction

The final stage of the writing process is going public. In this lesson students produce a final draft of their writing to share with an audience. In many class-rooms, "going public" means giving a piece of writing to the teacher to be read, scored, and returned. That's not very public! Kids' writing needs an audience. In our classroom each child takes home a book of paragraphs the other students have written based on that child's president interview. That's a pretty terrific purpose and audience. All other finalized pieces in our room go public as well, whether they are posted in the halls or bound into books. If my students work hard and effectively throughout the process, they deserve to have their work read by many. What a powerful message for the kids when they see other students and adults stopping in the hall to read their work!

MENTOR TEXTS FOR TEACHERS

- Harvey Daniels and Steven Zemelman's *Content-Area Writing: Every Teacher's Guide* (2007)
- Judy Davis and Sharon Hill's *The No-Nonsense Guide to Teaching Writing: Strategies, Structures, Solutions* (2003)
- Ralph Fletcher and JoAnn Portalupi's *Writing Workshop: The Essential Guide* (2001)
- Shelley Harwayne's *Writing Through Childhood: Rethinking Process and Product* (2001)

MATERIALS
- Revised and edited drafts (students)
- Lined paper (or computers for word processing) (students)

TIME: 30 minutes.

Here's How It Goes

"Some of the paragraphs we write this year are going to be bound into a book that I'll give to the student who was president the week we wrote them and that are therefore based on his or her interview; they need to be perfect. Some of our work will go up out in the hall for everyone to see—students and adults. And some will be just for our class, but it still needs to be done neatly and correctly. Can you imagine if I published a book that was full of errors? No one would buy it—plus my editors wouldn't allow it. As your teacher, I'm your editor, and I won't allow it. If I tell you this year that we're finalizing a piece, that means no errors.

"Now you get to write the final draft of your piece. Appearance is important, as is making sure you correct the errors you found in your draft. When you're done, I'd like you to read it aloud to yourself to double-check it. Remember, our ears can catch errors that our eyes can't."

Students may finalize their piece on the computer or write it out by hand. As the year progresses, the students discover the advantage of word processing—their drafts are saved as electronic files, and revision and editing are much easier. If students word process at home, they either bring in a printed copy to revise/edit in class or attach the efile to an email and I print it out. Figures 1.10 and 1.11 are examples of students' work.

Getting to this final stage takes a week of instruction, but I introduce both the writing process and how to construct a paragraph. It's a gradual, step-by-step progression, and I provide feedback every step of the way. This is part of "going slow to go fast"—if I model it well, the next time we practice, we pick up the pace!

Pressing Your Advantage

Students need immediate feedback about their writing, whether in connection with a rubric or as a short written response from you. (Rule of thumb: Kids should receive feedback on their writing within two days to make it meaningful!) When students receive prompt feedback, they know their work is important. They are

Figure 1.10 A student's handwritten draft of a narrative based on the stories I shared.

Has your dog ever had a face full of porcupine quills? Mrs. B's. dog has. When Mrs. Blauman was pregnant with her son John, she, her husband Eric, and her 4 year old daughter Carolynn went camping in Eagle camp. They camped out in the wild. Mrs. Blauman brought her dogs Bandit and Cassidy. They unleashed the dogs. Next thing you know, Bandit starts barking. Eric follows the barking. He laughs.
    "Bandit No!"
They came back. Bandit tried to bite a porcupine! His face was covered in porcupine quills. They tried to pull them out with tweezers but they couldn't, so they drove all the way to Keystone to get pliers. They still couldn't get them out! After that, they drove to Denver. They took Bandit to the Vet for surgery. Know you know about Bandit and the porcupine.

by Bennett

Figure 1.11 Colton's letter of recommendation on a classmate. Notice the persuasive aspects!

May 11, 2011

To Whom It May Concern:

It's been my pleasure to know Cooper. I've known him almost my whole life. Cooper is an athletic, smart, and nice person. This is what I like the most about Cooper.

He is athletic because he bikes, plays soccer, swims, and plays football. He bikes on the Christian Biking Club all year except for winter and fall. The Panthers is the name of his soccer team. Cooper plays pass with the football with his brother. And he has been swimming for 3 years.

Cooper is a good student because he gets all of his homework and projects in on time. He also makes good grades. He will help others with their work when they need it. Cooper is never late to class. He studies and prepares for tests. He understands all of his work and enjoys doing it.

Cooper is nice because he helps others and makes sure their ok. He is respectful to his teachers and classmates. He will share many of his materials. Cooper plays electric guitar. He likes to play the instrument even though he's not in a band. I think most musical people are nice.

Cooper is a good friend. His athletic, academic, and nice personality is the reason I like Cooper. I hope this information helps you to know Cooper better. I think you will agree with me.

Sincerely,
Colton

---

also able to reflect on the feedback and apply it to their next piece of writing. Wait too long and the kids forget what they've written.

When I was a student, I turned a final paper in to the teacher and then received the marked-up paper back with a grade. Only the teacher read it, and I would judge its merit by how little red ink there was. If there was a lot of red ink bleeding off the page, I knew I had failed. I never write on a student's final draft.

Ever. If a student turns in a piece that is not ready to be published, we finalize it together, but the student marks it up.

When the Kids Don't Get It

What about special-needs kids? Do I put papers with errors in the hall? No. I confer with students about their editing, make sure they correct all errors (with my help), and type up the final pieces for my students who really struggle with handwriting.

One-to-One

Alexa and I have worked together on her editing, and all she needed to do was recopy it; however, she has recopied the same errors she made on her first draft. Although she has written neatly, she hasn't paid attention to all the work we've done. I need to be explicit with her—right now, at the beginning of the year—that if you take a piece through the entire process and want it ready for an audience, it needs to be perfect (or as close to perfect as possible).

Me: I appreciate how you took your time to write this neatly, but I have to ask you: Do you think this is an acceptable final draft? Is it perfect?

Alexa: Well, it looks nice.

Me: Yes, but remember how I helped you edit it? Remember how we sat together and added periods and corrected spelling? Did you fix those when you copied it as a final? Are all the words spelled correctly?

Alexa: Well, no.

Me: Is this acceptable in our class—is it ready for an audience?

Alexa: I guess not.

Me: So what do you think I'm going to ask you to do? Because I want this to represent your best effort.

Alexa: Do I have to recopy it again?

Me: Yes. I know that's tough, but if we've worked this hard on the process, we need to be able to take pride in the product. Sometimes it takes a little bit more time to do it right, but that's usually better than having to spend the time to redo it again.

This is a hard lesson to impart, but we have to hold kids accountable! And students generally only need to learn this lesson once.

Owning the Lesson

If students take the time and effort to take a piece through the entire writing process, we need to value their writing. They need feedback (rubrics and comments) and an audience. Having their peers read their work is powerful. Posting final writing in the hall for others to read is powerful. Including it in newsletters and publications is powerful. We want our students to realize the power of their words.

Questions to Think About

- How often do my students finalize their writing?
- How do my students share their writing and make it public?
- Do my students know the audience for and the purpose of their writing?
- Do my students get to assess or reflect on their writing? Do they get to score their writing using rubrics?
- What type of feedback do I give my students?
- How timely is my feedback?

Wrap-Up

This first cluster of lessons shows how I teach my students to write various types of paragraphs. If I have twenty-five students, the ritual spans twenty-six weeks (because I'm interviewed, too). In these first lessons I demonstrate the writing process and set up the writing workshop. As we progress, my students do most of their president paragraph writing at home, and we use our writing workshop for other projects. Students learn to write like writers. They also meet most of the Common Core writing standards in an authentic context. At the end of the year, I ask the kids to reflect on what helped/what they remember. Here's what two fourth graders had to say:

> Writing was my favorite thing this year. For years I was afraid to write well because I was afraid of being made fun of. Now I've been writing well and my family is proud of me. Writing has become a part of me. Writing is very important now that I've learned that writing is a part of life.
>
> –Ryan

> At the beginning of the year as a reader I only saw myself as a reader, not a writer. Now as a reader I see myself as a good reader **and** writer. At the beginning of the year I loved to read and still do, but I hated writing. Now I love both. The president paragraphs helped and not giving writing sheets helped too. Also when you opened your mind to us it helped and how you read the books. I enjoyed how you gave us lots of free time to read in the day.
>
> –Ellie

The Powerful Benefits of the President Ritual

Students:

- Take two-column notes
- Organize their notes
- Build community (they learn a lot about me)
- Are introduced to modeling (they know what to do when they're president)
- Speak and take risks in front of their classmates (it's tough to get up and share for some)
- Become familiar with the writing process: planning (note taking and highlighting), drafting, revising, editing, publishing
- Develop revision techniques and learn how to revise with peers
- Become familiar with editing expectations (spelling, punctuation, etc.)
- Write narrative paragraphs (if that's been my focus)
- Write descriptive/informational/explanatory paragraphs (if that's been my focus)
- Write persuasive/opinion paragraphs (if that's been my focus)
- Write for an audience
- Develop writing stamina

What About Assessment?

I use rubrics to score my students' writing. For long-term work within a large unit of study I use the six-traits writing rubric, because it covers ideas and content, organization, word choice, sentence fluency, voice, and grammar and conventions. For these president paragraphs, though, I use Colorado's holistic four-point rubric, because that is how my students will be scored on short writing responses on state tests. I want my students to *internalize* that rubric and understand exactly what is expected of them to earn a proficient score *and then to push themselves to go beyond the rubric*. If my bedrock expectation is that my students will do the best work possible, I want to be explicit about how they can accomplish this.

How Does This Work When the Kids Are President?

If I am teaching fourth through sixth grades, I expect the paragraphs to be drafted and finalized at home. Note taking, revision, and editing are all done at school. However, I also make time for students who need extra time and support (or who are unable to complete assigned work at home) to create drafts and prepare final copies at school.

▶ **THE NITTY-GRITTY**

An in-depth look at this is included in Appendices A and B.

What Else?

I embed and practice specific writing workshop skills in the president paragraph work. If we are studying strong verbs, I ask students to include strong verbs in their drafts. On revision day we highlight strong verbs in one color, passive verbs in another, and then we work on making the passive ones more powerful. Or we may focus on figurative language, and I'll require students to use a simile in one of the paragraphs. If we're learning how to craft sentences, I'll require students to vary sentences in their paragraphs. I use these weekly paragraphs as a way to teach the elements of strong writing. What skills are you responsible for teaching in your writing curriculum? Can you embed them in these paragraphs? Here's a brief list to get you started:

- Verbs
- Sentence structure/sentence fluency
- Word choice (strong vocabulary, specificity)
- Transitions
- Similes
- Metaphors
- Personification
- Alliteration
- Concluding sentences

Things to Think About

Now that you've finished this section, consider what you can take away, suss out, and adapt for your own classroom. Even if you don't incorporate president paragraphs, think about how you could use the basic lesson formats.

- How could you embed these lessons into your writing workshop to teach the writing process?

- What types of paragraph writing do you teach?

- How can you use the concept of mentor texts to enhance writing instruction?

Instilling a Love of Language, Word Play, Vocabulary, and Poetry

6. Discovering New Words in the Context of Beautiful Language
7. Letting Poetry Teach Kids
8. Lifting Lines from Mentor Texts
9. Writing Poetry

I love to start the year with vocabulary, because it so obviously colors all content-area learning. Words give us power, and kids want power. That may seem a rather Donald Trumpian way to state it, but it rings true. They also want *motion*, momentum: Watch them gyrating on the playground or sports field; bouncing from couch to chair to floor in the living room; jockeying to win the board game, be the best friend, get a laugh; or jumping into a book conversation, yearning to have their insight make big waves.

Their kinetic energy informs how we frame our teaching. We need to give their intellectual energy the same freedom to bounce around, not slow them down for no reason. When it comes to building vocabulary, I think students are indeed being tripped up and blockaded unnecessarily—textbooks that are tough to parse, bad book matches, not enough word-attack skills under their belt to be able to solve unfamiliar words, and so on.

The lessons in this section help students embrace words by recognizing their power and using rich language to enhance all they do in school. The lessons encompass vocabulary, beautiful language, and the power of poetry. I also show you how to use the writer's notebook and quick-writes to move your writing workshop forward. But it all starts with vocabulary.

Building vocabulary in the content areas is also integral to building background knowledge and being able to understand new concepts, so I spend a lot of time front-loading vocabulary in math, science, and social studies and having students commit these new terms to memory. Memorization is the key. Skill-and-drill vocabulary worksheets don't do the trick. Neither does writing vocabulary words in sentences. William Nagy's research (1988) shows that learning vocabulary hinges on connecting new words to something that allows you to lock them into your long-term memory.

From the first week of school we notice words. Initially I model the process. I notice words in our reading, I notice words in our writing, and we discuss them. I love words, and that passion is contagious. Words are part of literacy study, and I want my students to love the language.

Unlike Lesson Cluster One, these lessons can also stand on their own. Whether in the context of learning a specific skill or applying these skills within president paragraphs, students authentically practice using precise, beautiful language.

Aligning Your Instruction with the Common Core State Standards

Many of the lessons in this section deal with poetry. Although poetry is not emphasized in the writing portion of the standards, studying poetry teaches students how to choose and use words wisely to communicate. Rich words. Specific words. New words. With that thought in mind—that poetry helps us teach craft and structure—I list the anchor standards for language first. The reading and writing standards are also a huge focus of these lessons, because students use mentor texts to improve the quality of their writing.

COLLEGE AND CAREER READINESS ANCHOR STANDARDS FOR LANGUAGE

KNOWLEDGE OF LANGUAGE

1. Apply knowledge of language to understand how language functions in different contexts, to make effective choices for meaning or style, and to comprehend more fully when reading or listening.

In these lessons students read a variety of mentor texts in different genres. They notice how language varies from poetry to narrative to persuasive and informative nonfiction. The lessons on beautiful language, sensory language, and figurative language address this topic specifically.

VOCABULARY ACQUISITION AND USE

2. Determine or clarify the meaning of unknown and multiple-meaning words and phrases by using context clues, analyzing meaningful word parts, and consulting general and specialized reference materials, as appropriate.

3. Demonstrate understanding of figurative language, word relationships, and nuances in word meanings.

4. Acquire and use accurately a range of general academic and domain-specific words and phrases sufficient for reading, writing, speaking, and listening at the college and career readiness level; demonstrate independence in gathering vocabulary knowledge when encountering an unknown term important to com-prehension or expression.

These three standards are front and center in the lessons that follow. I begin with lessons on the power of words and vocabulary. New vocabulary is a key component throughout. Learning how to use words—nuances, figurative language, specific terms—gives students' written communication even more power.

COLLEGE AND CAREER READINESS ANCHOR STANDARDS FOR WRITING

PRODUCTION AND DISTRIBUTION OF WRITING

5. Produce clear and coherent writing in which the development, organization, and style are appropriate to task, purpose, and audience.

6. Develop and strengthen writing as needed by planning, revising, editing, rewrit-ing, or trying a new approach.

7. Use technology, including the Internet, to produce and publish writing and to interact and collaborate with others.

The lessons included in this section go from drafting all the way through finalizing,

RANGE OF WRITING

8. Write routinely over extended time frames (time for research, reflection, and revision) and shorter time frames (a single sitting or a day or two) for a range of tasks, purposes, and audiences.

The only way we can help students build writing stamina is to give them plenty of time and practice. The more opportunities they have to study writers and practice writing like writers—writing for authentic purposes—the more proficient they will become.

COLLEGE AND CAREER READINESS ANCHOR STANDARDS FOR READING

CRAFT AND STRUCTURE

9. Interpret words and phrases as they are used in a text, including determining technical, connotative, and figurative meanings, and analyze how specific word choices shape meaning or tone.

10. Analyze the structure of texts, including how specific sentences, paragraphs, and larger portions of the text (e.g., a section, chapter, scene, or stanza) relate to each other and the whole.

11. Assess how point of view or purpose shapes the content and style of a text.

These standards mesh beautifully with the knowledge-of-language standard. Let's give our students the power of words and also the ability to deconstruct texts and apply their learning to their own writing. Although learning new vocabulary is powerful, taking reading and comprehension to a deeper level by understanding figurative language, analyzing how it affects meaning or tone, and then using it in our writing merges reading and writing with few seams. Examining poetry, students will analyze stanzas and relate the pieces of the poem to the whole. Understanding point of view and purpose are also embedded in these lessons.

RANGE OF READING AND LEVEL OF TEXT COMPLEXITY

12. Read and comprehend complex literary and informational texts independently and proficiently.

Mentor texts come in all sizes and shapes. By inviting students to join the search for great writing, we are asking them to bring in what they're reading—at a variety of levels. When we supply the text, we ensure that our students are exposed to complex literary and informational texts. The mentor texts I've included directly correspond to the reading standard—I include pieces across the content areas and at different reading levels. The key is to use anchor texts or foundational pieces (mentor texts) that are quality, that stretch our students, and that require them to think.

Lesson 6

Discovering New Words in the Context of Beautiful Language

(stands alone or is the foundation for lesson 7)

Introduction

I want my students to add new words to their speaking and writing repertoire, to feel empowered to use strong, rich language. Learning new words in the context of beautiful language is the basis for their being able to do so. This lesson scaffolds the ability to recognize new vocabulary words, which is important in the content areas. It also builds on the tracks-in-the-snow method for keeping track of student thinking and helps students to get into the habit of using dictionaries.

THE LANGUAGE OF LEARNING

"Tracks in the snow" is a metaphor for ink on paper used by Stephanie Harvey and Anne Goudvis in *Strategies That Work* (2000). So often we ask our students to write in response to reading (also part of the Common Core State Standards [CCSS]). It can be as simple as jotting notes or codes on sticky notes or bookmarks or in the white space (the "snow") around the text. These "tracks" are short bursts of thinking, not necessarily in sentence form, that give you a glimpse into your students' thinking—why they think the way they do. And because they're short, all your students can join in! (Alternate metaphors are tracks in the sand or tracks in the mud, depending on your geographic region and what the students understand!) Do I use tracks in the snow as informal assessments? Absolutely. I can collect them and determine student understanding. More often I have students keep all their "tracks" in their writing folders, ready to be referred to.

MENTOR TEXTS FOR STUDENTS

- Stephen R. Jones and Ruth Carol Cushman's *Colorado Nature Almanac: A Month-by-Month Guide to Wildlife and Wild Places* (Pruett, 1998) integrates both Colorado science and social studies into my literacy classroom. There are beautifully written books addressing the topography, geography, history, and so on of every state. A visit to your local bookstore or an Internet search to find a book about the state you teach in is time well spent.

- The ten volumes of Joy Hakim's *A History of US* (Oxford University Press, 2007), on U.S. history, are beautifully written and any of them lend themselves to this lesson. Additionally, the series is included in the CCSS appendix on books for a range of reading and they integrate beautifully with the history/social studies standards.

- *National Geographic* articles. I use articles from the adult magazine as well as articles from *National Geographic for Kids*. These are easily adaptable for use with SMART Boards.

MATERIALS FOR STUDENTS

- A richly written, descriptive text (one copy per student) that can be integrated with social studies or science (e.g., *Colorado Nature Almanac*); choose one that will push your students, that includes new vocabulary

- Pencils

- Two different-color highlighters per student

- Writer's notebook

- Dictionaries

TIME: 1 hour

Here's How It Goes

"We've been looking at Colorado animals, and now I want to show you a piece about Colorado." I hold up the book *Colorado Nature Almanac*. "I fell in love with this book because the chapters are the months of the year, and each chapter discusses what happens that month in the natural world in Colorado. And the first page of each chapter is beautifully written. You know how we're working on descriptive writing? Well, this is an example of awesome descriptive writing. What month are we in right now?"

"September, of course," Naomi observes wryly.

"Yep, so I pulled the September piece. But because this is such a tough piece and this is the first time we've done this, I'm going to read it as a think-aloud. You guys all get your copy and I'll put mine on the doc camera and model. Want to have a go?"

The students collect their copies, go back to their seats, and get out highlighters and pencils.

"Okay, I'm going to be looking for two things. I want to notice new vocabulary—words I don't know—and I'm going to highlight them with one color. I think I'll code that—leave tracks in the snow—by making a mark in that color at the top of the page and then writing *vocab* next to it. Can you do that for me too? Pick any color and make a key on your paper.

"The second reason why I want to read this piece is its beautiful language. I want to notice what the authors do to help me visualize or create sensory images. So I'm going to take my other highlighter and add one more thing to the key. I'm going to put a dab of that color here and write *beautiful language*. Would you do that please?"

I turn back to the piece on the document camera and begin to read the first paragraph. "I'm going to code when I find beautiful language. I really like this line that says, 'Ladybugs come together in bright orange clusters on mountaintops.' I can visualize that clearly, but I'm also wondering why ladybugs are on mountaintops—I'm kind of thinking that they'd die up there, so this line surprises me. I'm going to highlight that with the color I chose for beautiful language and then I'm going to leave tracks in the snow and write in the margin, 'Surprises me—I can see this. Don't they die that high?' If other lines strike you in that paragraph, highlight them." (An example of a student's coded text is shown in Figure 2.1.)

"I'm also betting there's a word in this paragraph that you don't know. Skim through on your own and see whether a word jumps out at you that you don't know."

Emma's hand immediately goes up. "*Wafts*. I don't know the word *wafts*."

"Nice job, Emma. We are also working on vocabulary today—see, I have this chart ready." I have chart paper prepared at the front of the room so we can co-construct a class anchor chart (see Figure 2.2). "And I'm betting that some of you will notice that it

Figure 2.1 The First Page of "September" as Coded by a Student

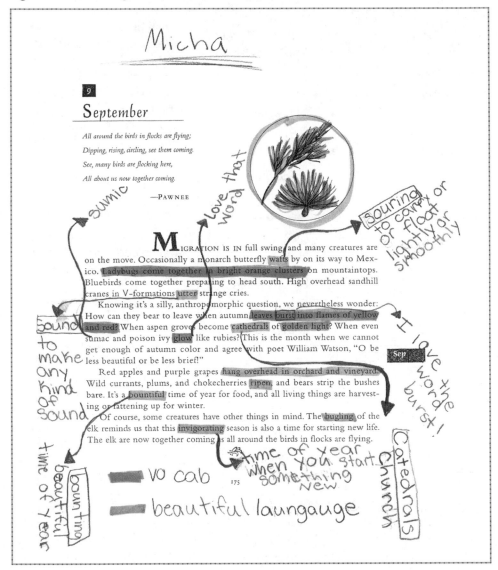

looks like our vocabulary chart in our book lover's book [BLB]. Today I'm going to start modeling what we'll be doing in that section. So I'm going to write, 'September/175' under *Piece/Page* and then I'm going to write the word *wafts*. The next column is headed *Part of Speech/Think It Means*—let's take a stab at this word using the context.

"Before we do that, though, what part of speech do you think it is?"

Dexter's hand flies up. "A verb?"

Figure 2.2 Vocabulary Anchor Chart

Piece/ Page	Word	Part of Speech/ Think It Means	Actual Meaning (Dictionary)	Ways to Remember (Long Term)
"September"/ 175	Wafts	v. –flies by –flutters –soars beautifully –goes by swiftly	v., to carry or float smoothly or lightly	Think of butterflies; imagine the aroma coming from a pie
	Invigorating	adj. –mating –transitional –warm –overwhelming	adj., filled with life and energy	Picture a hot tub and then an ice plunge
	Utter	v. –moan –yelp –screech –cry out	v., to give an audible sound	Think of a face with a speech bubble coming from the mouth

"Why?"

"Because it's an action."

I write down *v.* and then record what the kids think it might mean.

"Now we need to find the actual meaning. I'm going to use the dictionary. But I need to know, do I look up *waft* or *wafts*?" The kids answer, and we get the definition written and confirm the part of speech. Finally I point to the fifth column.

"This is the most important column, because it indicates how you will get the word to transfer to your long-term memory. We either need to create a picture to help us remember or make a connection to solidify it for us." We discuss pictures and ways to remember and I sketch them in the last column. Figure 2.3 shows a student's work on a similar chart in his BLB.

Figure 2.3 The Vocabulary Section of a Student's BLB

Text/Page number	WORD	What I think it means	Actual Meaning (Dictionary)	Ways to Remember
September piece	wafts	fly, drifts	to float lightly	butterfly 🦋
11	anthropomorphic	NO Idea	giving human form or attributes to a non-human thing	morph = change
11	bountiful	beautiful, amazing, bouncing	plentiful, abundant (a lot)	feast! Thanksgiving
Molly Moon's	engrossed	filled, wanted	to occupy completely or absorb	Spongebob
11	initiative	independence	ones personal descision	independence
11	coveted	great, amazing	something that belongs to another	not yours
11	persuaded	talked person into it	to convince	force
11	dehydrated	tired	to lose liquids or water	hydrated
End Game	irritable	annoying	easily annoyed	irritated
11	abundance	amount	plenty, enough	a lot abundance
11	grattified	old	to give pleasure to	generous.
11	voids	groups	an empty space	emptiness

CCSS, *GRADE BY GRADE*

This lesson supports the CCSS requirement of studying vocabulary in context beautifully. You can use this lesson to meet Language standards 4 and 6 easily. With a little fine-tuning, you can also meet Language standard 5!

Third grade: Addressing roots and affixes will ensure that all elements of L.3.4 are met. If you explicitly discuss shades of meaning and the differences between literal and nonliteral meanings of words, you'll have L.3.5 covered, too!

Fourth and fifth grade: To meet all of the pieces of L.4.4 and L.5.4, look for examples of Greek and Latin affixes and roots in the words students identify. Help students to use these word parts to determine the meanings of the words they've chosen. To support students' mastery of L.4.5 and L.5.5, encourage students to identify idioms, adages, and proverbs as well as individual new words. Consider adding synonym and antonym columns to their vocabulary notes.

Sixth grade: In addition to the modifications above for fourth and fifth grade, add a "Relationships" column to the students' vocabulary list. In this column, challenge students to identify the relationships between words (e.g., part/whole, item/category) and to use words' connotations to differentiate between words with similar meanings.

▶ **THE NITTY-GRITTY**

This is also a lesson on how to use the dictionary, where I model and do most of the work (gradual release). A document camera is an excellent tool—I can put the dictionary directly beneath it and show guide words, entries, definition, part of speech, and so on. Students definitely require more direct instruction, but they are exposed to the dictionary as a tool (which is part of the CCSS!).

» **USING TECHNOLOGY**

I model with a document camera in this lesson, but you can just as easily project the piece on a SMART Board. And you can find tons of examples on the Internet. Invite students to join the search. If they notice a well-written article, capture the Web address and use it!

We continue with this process for vocabulary and language paragraph by paragraph, noticing beautiful language and vocabulary such as *anthropomorphic*. In the final paragraph the word *invigorating* jumps out as a word to include on the chart.

▶ **THE NITTY-GRITTY**

I always have the kids put their coded texts in their writing folders, so they'll be able to refer to them later.

Pressing Your Advantage: Moving to Quick Writes (*about 20 minutes*)

Once I've modeled my coding of the text and the students have marked theirs, it's time to use this piece as a mentor text—a well-written piece to trigger our own writing. If I have time the same day and if my students have the stamina to continue working, I do this immediately. If I run out of time or the students lose focus, I do it the following day.

"You guys have noticed so much about this piece. Let's take out our writer's notebooks and do a ten-minute quick-write. What I mean by that is that we're going to write for ten minutes—not *think* for ten minutes, but actually write. These authors have given us a lot to write about. They've used beautiful, descriptive language—you could try that. You could also try poetry. You could write about the month of September and anything connected to it. Or you could pull a word from the text and try using just that. For example, I'm thinking that I'm going to play with the word *wafts*. I'll be writing with you for the first five minutes, then I'll get up and move around the room. Remember, ten minutes of writing."

THE LANGUAGE OF LEARNING

Although students of course add new vocabulary to their individual word lists, a class word wall is also a tremendous way to capture and record new words. Each week students can choose one word they think is worthy of adding to the wall. Have them write it on a sentence strip and add their own definition (and in many cases a picture). This is incredibly beneficial for students who are just learning the English language. Word walls are also powerful ways to teach content vocabulary.

We get out our writer's notebooks and start writing. I write with my students. I need them to *see* me as a writer. I also need to experience the same struggles that some of my students may face. Writing is one of the hardest skills for students to learn, so they need to see that I work hard at it too.

After five minutes, I get up and move around, reading over students' shoulders. This holds everyone accountable. I periodically stop for a quick question ("How did you do that?" [I'm truly curious]), or I work with a student who isn't writing.

After eight minutes, I tell them they need to finish up, that we're stopping in two minutes. Then I ask whether anyone would like to share. I've already shared some of my writing, so the kids know they'll be safe. Hands go up and I call on students. They stand by their desk and proudly share what they've written—description, poetry, humor. Each piece reflects that student and his or her connections to September. (See Figure 2.4.)

▶ **THE NITTY-GRITTY**

It's absolutely critical that I write along with the kids. If I sense that kids need a springboard, I'll read what I'm writing out loud, as a model. That way they know I'm working on the same thing they are, not writing my grocery list.

When Kids Don't Get It

Hays' hand goes up. "Just checking. It's September. September means football. This piece doesn't say anything about football, but I can connect football to September. Can I write about college football?"

"What do *you* think?"

Hays isn't used to that. He thinks for a moment then nods, "I guess if it makes sense."

"Hays, I'm so glad you asked, because this is about making connections. So if you can legitimately connect to this piece, go for it. My only stipulation is that you write for ten minutes."

One-to-One

As I'm walking around the room, glancing over shoulders, I notice that Luke has nothing on his page.

> **Me:** Whoa! It's already been five minutes and I don't see any writing on your page. How can that be?
>
> **Luke:** 'Cause there's nothing to write about.

▶ **THE NITTY-GRITTY**

My quick-writes are *uninterrupted*. Students may not get out of their seats to ask me questions. If they start to, they get "the hand"—I hold up my hand without looking at them—and they always return to their seats. I sit at a desk of an absent student, or I draw a stool up to a group of student desks, so I'm writing at the same level and part of the group.

Figure 2.4 Jonny first comes up with rhymes for *mating* (he spells it *maiting*). When he finishes, he moves on to a second piece more like a paragraph.

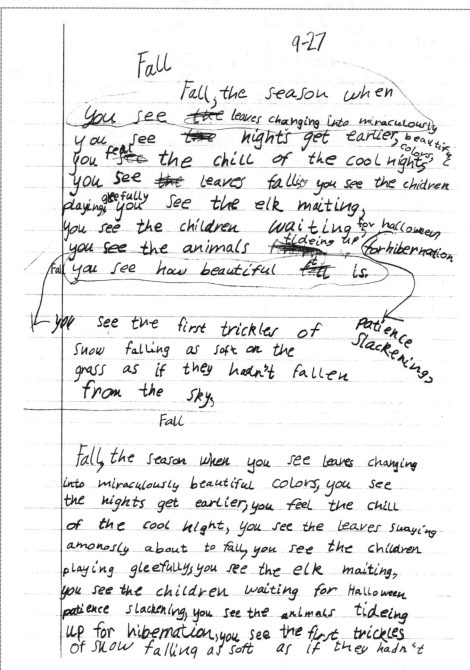

Me: You know that's a cop-out, we had lots of options. You could simply write about the month, you could try to use words from this piece, or you could work on description. The only expectation is that you write and that somehow it connects. What do you like to do in September? I know there are a lot of things you do when you're out of the classroom.

Luke: Broncos?

Me: Of course. Football season. Write about that. Where do you think you'll start?

Luke: The game this Sunday.

Me: Go. Get that pencil moving, because you know I'm coming back to check on you, right?

Luke: Yeah.

Me: And I'll want you to show me what you've written.

Luke already has the pencil moving and he knows I'll be back to check. No excuses. Everyone writes.

Owning the Lesson

This lesson introduces the concept of mentor texts. It has a dual track—students are reading and noticing what authors do with vocabulary and language, then writing using what they notice as a model or a springboard. How can you use mentor texts in your classroom to model exceptional writing? How can you use them to teach new vocabulary with the whole class? Can you replicate this lesson in other content areas (science, social studies, math)?

Questions to Think About

- Do my students notice new vocabulary?
- Do they use context clues to figure these words out?
- How do I know my students are using the dictionary independently and authentically?
- How do my students record and use new vocabulary?
- How do I bring language-rich writing to the forefront of my instruction?
- Who is in charge of noticing vocabulary and beautiful language, me or my students?
- How do I want students to transfer what they notice in mentor texts to their own writing?

Letting Poetry Teach Kids

Introduction

At the beginning of the year my focus is rich, deep language and strong vocabulary. Poets have to be choosey with words. Strong verbs and nouns abound. Figurative and sensory language is the norm. When reading poetry, students encounter countless wonderful aspects of writing! Instead of asking my students to complete worksheets, I give them a page of poetry and have them find examples of the elements of poetry I'm teaching. We notice whether great poetry uses active or passive verbs. We highlight and identify the figurative language. These pages, with their tracks in the snow, go into students' writer's notebooks, ready to be referred to when they want to write. I also make quick informal assessments as I walk through the room and glance over shoulders—I get a sense of who gets it and who needs more practice.

I want to start the year by laying the foundation for success, and even the most reluctant or impacted writers can connect with poetry successfully. Then I try to incorporate poems into my reading or writing workshops at least once a week, so that my students will enjoy and understand poetry.

MENTOR TEXTS FOR TEACHERS
- Ralph Fletcher's *Poetry Matters: Writing a Poem from the Inside Out* (2002)
- Donald Graves' *Explore Poetry* (1992)
- Georgia Heard's *For the Good of the Sun and the Earth: Teaching Poetry* (1989)

MENTOR TEXTS FOR STUDENTS

The key to successful poetry instruction is for students to have an abundance of available and accessible poetry books. Here are some suggestions:

- Douglas Florian's *Autumblings* (Greenwillow, 2003), *Insectlopedia* (Sandpiper, 2002), *In the Swim* (Harcourt, 1997), *Laugh-eteria* (Puffin, 1999), *Winter Eyes* (Greenwillow, 1999), *Mammalabilia* (Sandpiper, 2004), *Summersaults* (Greenwillow, 2002), *Handsprings* (Greenwillow, 2006), and *Comets, Stars, the Moon and Mars: Space Poems and Paintings* (Harcourt, 2007)

- Kristine O'Connell George's *Hummingbird Nest: A Journal of Poems* (Harcourt, 2004)

- Donald Graves' *Baseball, Snakes, and Summer Squash* (Wordsong, 1996)

- Eloise Greenfield's *Honey, I Love* (HarperCollins, 1978)

- David L. Harrison's *Somebody Catch My Homework* (Wordsong, 1993)

- Steven Schnur's *Autumn: An Alphabet Acrostic* (Clarion, 1997)

- Eileen Spinelli's *Here Comes the Year* (Henry Holt, 2002)

- Jane Yolen's *Water Music* (Boyds Mills, 1995), *Mother Earth, Father Sky: Poems of Our Planet* (Boyds Mills, 1996), *Once Upon Ice and Other Frozen Poems* (Boyds Mills, 1997), *Snow, Snow* (Boyds Mills, 1998), *Fine Feathered Friends: Poems for Young People* (Boyds Mills, 2004), *Color Me a Rhyme* (Boyds Mills, 2002), and *Horizons: Poems as Far as the Eye Can See* (Wordsong, 2002)

- Sheree Fitch's *No Two Snowflakes* (Orca, 2002)

- Barbara Rogasky's *Winter Poems* (Scholastic, 1999)

MATERIALS

- Copies for each student of short, accessible poems that exemplify the element of poetry or word study that will be the focus of the lesson (no more than three; you don't want to inundate them with too much text)

- Highlighters

- Pencils

- Chart paper

TIME: 35 to 40 minutes

Here's How It Goes

You can use this lesson to teach just about any aspect of poetry or word study. Here are a few ideas to get you started:

- Vocabulary
- Figurative language
- Strong verbs and nouns
- Imagery
- Inferences
- Sensory images
- Questions
- Specificity
- Precise word choices
- Line breaks
- Fluency

In this lesson, students notice personification. It can be adapted to teach other types of powerful language. In our study of figurative language, my students

THE LANGUAGE OF LEARNING

Here are short-and-sweet definitions of some of the types of figurative language:

Alliteration. Purposeful repetition of an initial sound (most often a consonant or consonant cluster) in two or more words or a phrase. (I also let students transfer this definition to the repetition of a middle or end sound.)

Hyperbole. Purposeful use of exaggeration to emphasize a point. Hyperbole should not be taken literally.

Metaphor. Creating a visual or sensory image in the reader's mind by comparing one thing to another without using the words *like* or *as*.

Onomatopoeia. Words that imitate the sound of the action or thing they represent. Cows *moo*. Sheep *baa*.

Personification. Giving human characteristics to anything not human.

Simile. Creating a visual or sensory image in the reader's mind by comparing one thing to another using the words *like* or *as*.

and I start the year noticing *onomatopoeia*, then move on to *alliteration*, followed by a study of *simile*, then *personification*, then *metaphor*, and possibly *hyperbole*. For this example, I'll show how I use this lesson to be sure that the kids "get" personification.

"I want to see how you do with finding personification on your own. You have done such an amazing job identifying it in books we've read. I have some poetry for you today and I want you to code it. I want you to highlight the personification and explain how it helps you visualize or create images. You might also jot down any other things you notice."

"Leave tracks in the snow," says Emma.

"Exactly. Try to figure out what the author means or why he's using personification. And of course leave me notes on what you notice about this poetry and the way it's written."

Depending on the complexity of the text, I might read it aloud with students, or I might let them read it on their own. Then the students begin to work independently. I sit down and mark the text as well. After a few minutes I start moving around the room, reading over students shoulders, making comments, nudging the "highlighting only" students to leave me tracks in the snow, and helping students who are struggling.

Students work at coding poetry, leaving "tracks in the snow."

THE LANGUAGE OF LEARNING

In a compass group, four students face each other like the four points of a compass—N, S, E, and W. For more information on teaching students how to listen, talk, and confer, see Chapter 7 in *The Inside Guide to the Reading–Writing Classroom*.

After ten or fifteen minutes, when most students seem to have finished, I say, "Now I would like you to form four-people compass groups and share your thinking, what you notice about these poems, what personification you see, what you like or don't like and why. After you're done sharing, we'll come back and talk together as a class."

Students move quickly into groups of four. As students discuss their thinking, I move from group to group and eavesdrop. I encourage groups who aren't using the dictionary to look up words to "get after it!" This is our way of working on dictionary skills authentically.

To finish up I call everyone back together. I ask each group to share key points, or I restate the ideas that I heard groups discussing. I want to label their thinking and give them credit. We use a class anchor chart to capture their thoughts. Anything important that isn't shared I teach explicitly.

Next, I want the kids to put what they've seen in the poem into their writing. "Now we're going to do a ten-minute quick-write. You may write anything you'd like, as long as it connects to the poems you've read. You may want to write something that uses personification. You may want to play with words the way that the poet did. You may want to write about the same topic as today's poem. It's your choice. I think I'm going to try using personification to capture the beauty of the season right now."

The students write for ten minutes, focusing on vocabulary, language, form, or an idea. (The quick-writes become fodder for future lessons when students create a final poem.) While the kids write, I take out my writer's notebook, find an empty seat, and write for five minutes. Then I get up and wander around the room, having quick conferences with students as I look over their shoulder. I always write with the students and often share what I'm writing to scaffold students who might not have ideas. Sometimes my writing comes fairly easily, sometimes I find

▶ THE NITTY-GRITTY

Why don't I offer comments after each child shares? First, time! I want the kids who feel comfortable sharing to have an opportunity. Second, I don't want any child to think I'm validating another student's work more than his or hers. Remember, these are quick-writes, not finished pieces, and I'm thrilled when kids are confident enough to stand and share. Sometimes there's more safety without the comments. When I'm walking around the room and reading over shoulders I often talk with individuals—commenting on what they're doing or what they've lifted from the text (which validates their work) or asking how they did that (and I truly want to know!). It's private but effective. And I always have students who double-check whether it's okay to take their notebooks home and continue to write. (Of course it is!)

I've picked a tough topic. Students need to see me struggle with writing, too. It doesn't always flow!

After eight minutes I warn them there are only two minutes left. After ten minutes we stop and many students share what they've written. This process goes quickly, because it's more sharing than conferring or asking questions or giving advice. I'm very careful not to give a lot of praise; I don't want to squelch anyone who might be afraid his or her work doesn't measure up.

Pressing Your Advantage

After we've studied a number of types of figurative language individually, I follow up with an informal assessment of students' knowledge of figurative language: "I want to see how you do with finding figurative language on your own. I have some poetry for you today, and I want you to highlight the figurative language and label it. Notice, I'm not telling you what you're looking for; I want to see if you know the types of figurative language."

You might want to customize the lesson even further by using picture books rather than poems. Choose a book with rich language (books by Jonathan London, Eve Bunting, Ralph Fletcher, Thomas Locker, Jane Yolen, Patricia Polacco, Chris Van Allsburg, and Cynthia Rylant are all excellent choices). I use *In November*, by Cynthia Rylant, to teach descriptive writing.

Once students are familiar with the process of hunting in a poem's text for ideas and support, you can teach inferring by presenting one of my students' favorite lessons, in which I use poems with the titles lopped off. I give kids copies of poems with the titles removed and ask them to use clues from the text to determine the title and *prove it* by highlighting the words in the text that help them figure it out. This lesson also reinforces the power of background knowledge when visualizing and inferring. Without schema to draw on, students can't figure out titles on their own. For example, "Magnifying Glass," by Valerie Worth (page 45 in *All the Small Poems and Fourteen More* (Farrar, Straus and Giroux, 1996)), is a stumper for kids (and adults, too); offering a clue (such as Sherlock Holmes) or having a magnifying glass in the room gives them a hook on which to hang their thinking. After we've done this activity once, my students beg to repeat "the poetry game."

When Kids Don't Get It

When you ask students to find personification (or verbs, or whatever) on their own, there will always be some who can't do it, who meet your directions with blank looks. Even after minilessons and practice, the concept hasn't sunk in. These students either don't get started or pretend, highlighting everything on the page in the hope that as you move around the room you'll think they know what they're doing. That's why their leaving tracks in the snow is so critical. When you notice students who don't understand the concept, pull them together for additional instruction and practice in a guided reading group.

One-to-One

Sometimes kids suffer from highlighter happiness, assuming that highlighting more makes them appear smarter. Quite the contrary. Just as I want my students to be choosey about the words they use, I want them to be choosey about their highlighting. Gina is giving her highlighter quite a workout, and I stop by her desk.

> **Me:** Wow! That's a lot of highlighting. Can you explain why you've highlighted all that?

> **Gina:** I think these show personification.

> **Me:** You said you *think*. Let's start there. Can you tell me what we decided personification was?

> **Gina:** I think it shows what a person is like.

> **Me:** Right. Can you give me an example? I think you've got the basic idea. Show me your thinking and then we can talk more.

> **Gina** [*hesitantly*]: "The winter sings."

> **Me:** Right. And I asked you guys to highlight examples of personification in these poems. Do you need a little help?

> **Gina:** I think so.

> **Me:** Why do you think this is personification? Can you tell me?

> **Gina:** Winter can't really sing, can it? People sing. Does that make that personification?

> **Me:** Yes. Now I want to know what that phrase makes you visualize or which of your senses it appeals to. Can you tell me a little more?

> **Gina:** Well, it hails in winter, but hail is noisy. And the next line helps me with how it sounds. Hey, there's a simile in the next line! It compares the sound of hail to the sound of nails falling. That means the song is really noisy.

> **Me:** Great thinking. The author got you thinking. Can you jot a few tracks in the snow there? [*Gina writes*, really noisy, ugly song.] I'm curious why you highlighted so much of this poem.

Gina: Well, I knew we were noticing personification, so I figured the whole poem was full of it.

Me: Interesting. So as we go through some of this together, what do you think?

Gina [*looking over the poem*]: That I shouldn't have highlighted so much. Can I get another-color highlighter out?

Me: Absolutely. Good problem solving. You ready to work on this a bit together?

And that's what we do. We read through part of the poem, identifying personification and talking about how it helps us create sensory images. Gina writes down a few tracks in the snow capturing her thinking. Then I let Gina tackle it on her own. Will I work with her some more on this? Absolutely. And if I had a handful of students who needed this lesson, I'd work with a small needs-based group instead of having individual conferences.

Owning the Lesson

This is a perfect time for you to check your curriculum and revisit what you have to teach. What aspects of grammar and language are part of your scope and sequence or the CCSS? What skills could you embed in this lesson, letting the kids do the work and earn their learning?

Questions to Think About

- What is my purpose for using a specific mentor text? What do I want students to learn or to do with it?
- Who is in charge of defining and explaining the poetry in my classroom?
- Do I pick a poetic form like the limerick, the acrostic, the haiku, and so on and explain it, or do I let kids "unwrap" how the author creates the form and then try it out for themselves?
- Do I use poetry to teach reading? Language? Vocabulary? Writing?
- Do my students have access to books of poetry? Are they exposed to a wide variety of poetry over an extended period of time?
- What else could I teach through poetry in an authentic way? Action verbs versus passive verbs? Sensory words? Vocabulary? How to use a thesaurus?

Lesson 8

Lifting Lines from Mentor Texts

Introduction

Books often contain powerful sentences that cry out to be used as examples. There are lots of great ways to demonstrate sentence fluency or show students how authors craft sentences. If I could take only one book with me to teach writing on a desert island, what would it be? Unequivocally, *Twilight Comes Twice*. It lends itself to both reading and writing. The visual imagery is beautiful, and Fletcher's sentence structure is precise and euphonious. Some years I read the book over two days: The first day we read about dusk, the next day we read about dawn. Some years I read it through in one sitting.

Often as writing teachers we encourage students to structure their sentences differently only to discover they don't know what to do. Using powerful sentences as examples is a great way to demonstrate sentence fluency or show students how authors craft sentences. Lifting lines is the perfect explicit exercise to encourage bite-size experiments with different techniques. Because the examples are then kept in students' writer's notebook, they can refer back to them to help transfer the technique to their writing.

THE LANGUAGE OF LEARNING

As you're reading to your students, look for sentences or lines that make you stop and say, "I wish I could write like that!" or "That is just the greatest sentence!" Any line that makes you take notice is worth mimicking and using as a model. Invite your kids on the search. Notice language and how words fit together. Find the sentences that surprise you.

I use this lesson throughout the year to give students a chance to "apprentice" themselves to great writers. The lines we lift are models students use to mimic structure and craft. This is a sophisticated lesson, but with a great model—and the opportunity to take risks—students will attempt things they wouldn't do on their own.

MENTOR TEXT FOR TEACHERS

- Natalie Goldberg's *Writing Down the Bones* (2010) is a terrific resource for teaching writing. A line from it that captures the idea of mentor texts: "If you read good books, when you write, good books will come out of you."

MENTOR TEXTS FOR STUDENTS

- Ralph Fletcher's *Twilight Comes Twice* (Clarion, 1997) and *Hello, Harvest Moon* (Clarion, 2003)

- Eileen Spinelli's *My Mama Had a Dancing Heart* (Orchard Paperbacks, 1999)

- Sheree Fitch's *No Two Snowflakes* (Orca, 2002)

▶ THE NITTY-GRITTY

The more we can share about authors and how they write—go about their craft—the more authentic writing becomes for our students. There are particular authors whom I go to every year. I can count on their books to give my students a solid foundation in writing craft, especially word choice and sentence structure. I bring in biographies or autobiographies. I encourage students to join the search. They become masters at finding new information on the Internet, printing it off, and posting it on a section of the bulletin board entitled Meet the Author.

THE LANGUAGE OF LEARNING

Natalie Goldberg (2010) comments:

> Writers are great lovers. They fall in love with other writers. That's how they learn to write. They take on a writer, read everything by him or her, read it over again until they understand how the writer moves, pauses and sees. . . . Your ability to love another's writing means those capabilities are awakened in you. It will only make you bigger; it won't make you a copy cat. The parts of another's writing that are natural to you will become you, and you will use some of those moves when you write. . . . So writing is not just writing. It is also having a relationship with other writers.

That's why we use mentor texts. We want our students to fall in love with other writers, to read and study.

- Thomas Locker's *Water Dance* (Voyager, 1997), *The Man Who Paints Nature* (Richard C. Owens, 1999), *Cloud Dance* (Voyager, 2003), *Sky Tree* (HarperCollins, 2001), and *Home* (Sandpiper, 2000)
- Several titles from prolific authors such as Jonathan London, Patricia Polacco, Cynthia Rylant, and Jane Yolen

MATERIALS

- *Twilight Comes Twice*, by Ralph Fletcher (I do this lesson repeatedly throughout the year with a variety of other well-written texts; by all means, choose your own favorite)
- Chart paper
- Highlighters
- Writer's notebook (students)

TIME: 45 minutes (book study could be a part of writing workshop for a week)

Here's How It Goes

After we've read and savored the book, I pull out one sentence and put it on the board for students to try to replicate in their writer's notebook. (I use the one below because it creates a vivid image and begins with an adverb. You will of course use any sentence that strikes you and meets your purpose.)

> Slowly dusk pours
> the syrup of darkness
> into the forest. (p. 11)

"While I read, you guys wrote down words and lines that struck you. You can go back to these and use them in your own writing. But sometimes writers practice by trying to mimic another author's style—especially how they write sentences. I call that *lifting lines*, and I want us to practice with this one.

"I specifically chose this line because we are working on how sentences are constructed and a lot of you are asking how you can change your sentences around. Look at how Fletcher starts this sentence. What do you notice?"

Rebecca immediately answers, "The first word ends in *-ly*."

"Exactly. What part of speech is that? We've talked about it."

The kids sit and think for a moment and I'm wondering if I'm going to have to tell them. Finally Bennett raises his hand and asks, "Adverbs?"

"Yep. So I want you to try to write *at least* three descriptive sentences that start with adverbs. Let's brainstorm a few adverbs so we have some choices."

The kids throw out *quickly, immediately, swiftly, hurriedly,* and *tiredly.*

To further scaffold their success, I write down a practice sentence on the anchor chart: *Suddenly, the black clouds open and a bucket of water douses me.* "What am I talking about?"

"Thunderstorms!"

I write down another: *Silently the powdered sugar drifts from the sky, coating the ground in shimmering white.* "What's that one?"

"Snow, of course!"

I wind up the lesson, "Think you can try it? Let's give it a whirl. I'll write with you for five minutes, then walk around to see how you're doing."

The kids get to work. As I'm writing in my journal, I stop and share my examples so the kids will be sure to understand. *Quickly the clouds roll in like angry waves hitting the shore; one wall of gray after another.* And: *Slowly the sun's rays emerge from among the clouds like a butterfly emerging from its chrysalis one golden wing at a time.* Writing with the kids, I experience the task as well: if I've assigned something really difficult, I know it! (See Figure 2.5 for an example of a student's notebook.)

Trinity writes:

Gently, swallowed by clouds afloat in the winter sky. Landing in the most strange of places they dance down. Catch them, but they tingle your

▶ THE NITTY-GRITTY

Do I always look for sentences that start with adverbs? No. It depends on my purpose. What do you want the kids to learn? What do they need in their writing? What are examples of phenomenal text? The sky is the limit in terms of what can be taught by lifting a single sentence or several sentences. Some possibilities are:

- All types of figurative language
- Compound sentences
- Complex sentences
- Clauses
- Beginning sentences with participles (*-ing* words)
- Tenses (past, present, future)
- Vivid verbs/action verbs
- All types of punctuation
- Speeding up the pace or slowing it down (using commas in a list speeds it up, repetition slows the pace down) (Rylant is a master at slowing down the pace!)
- Repetition
- Breaking the rules (beginning sentences with *and* or *but,* for example) and discussing *why* an author breaks the rule
- Transitions
- Varying sentence length

Figure 2.5 Jonny's Writer's Notebook

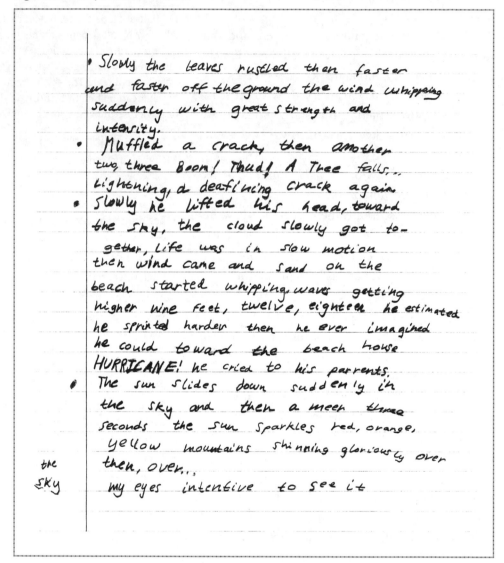

- Slowly the leaves rustled then faster and faster off the ground the wind whipping suddenly with great strength and intensity.
- Muffled a crack, then another two, three Boom! Thud! A Tree falls, lightening, a deafening crack again
- Slowly he lifted his head, toward the sky, the cloud slowly got together, life was in slow motion then wind came and sand on the beach started whipping, waves getting higher nine feet, twelve, eighteen he estimated he sprinted harder then he ever imagined he could toward the beach house HURRICANE! he cried to his parrents.
- The sun slides down suddenly in the sky and then a meer three seconds the sun sparkles red, orange, yellow mountains shinning gloriously over then, over...
the sky   my eyes intentive to see it

tongue, and your hearts. Beginning to fall harder, quickly prepare for if you don't you shall miss Mother Nature's kiss. Swiftly the crystals stop, you look down from the sky and see the picture they have painted and know it will drift away leaving a fall painting in its place. But know it is here so enjoy it because this magical day only comes once, and that is if you are dreaming.

Dexter is briefer and shows his sense of humor:

> Slowly Jello jiggles all over the floor. Loudly mom says "what a mess!" Quietly the boy snickers, "Ha Ha." Suddenly the dog eats it up.

As I move about the room, glancing over student's shoulders, I'm looking especially for kids who aren't using adverbs, so I can step in and teach. I generally suggest some "easy" adverbs (*quietly, softly, suddenly*) and a couple of topics (weather and sports are good ones). (See the following One-to-One for an example.)

Pressing Your Advantage

We return to the text on following days, noticing and labeling the figurative language Fletcher uses and the images he creates. Or I may have each student take their highlighter and choose one sentence she or he would like to practice replicating.

I revisit this book throughout the school year, using it to teach different writing components. Inevitably, at the end of the school year when I ask students to reflect on their writing and to share specific books that influenced them as writers, this title shows up big time.

When Kids Don't Get it

Generally I notice students who aren't getting it as I circulate and read over shoulders. Often a brief conference helps. But if I have students who still struggle with this concept, I might pull a group together to reinforce adverbs (or whatever else is the purpose of the lesson). Instead of finding the adverbs myself, though, I have the students do the noticing—finding the *-ly* words in a piece of text and then discussing what those words do (what part of speech they are). This might also be homework—"In your independent reading at home, pay attention and put a sticky note on the page where you find a sentence beginning with an *-ly* word and bring it in to share with the group tomorrow." The more I turn the search over to the students, the better it sinks in.

▶ **THE NITTY-GRITTY**

What's the difference between "lifting" and plagiarizing? Think about how published authors become good writers—they write, and they use other authors as mentors. Authors often state that they practiced crafting sentences like the authors they wanted to emulate. We notice what great authors do, then we try it in our own writing. We take a word or a short phrase from a piece and play with it in our own writing. We appropriate a simile but change the words or tweak it to fit a new idea. We notice how sentences are constructed and we try that construction in our own writing. Lifting isn't copying—it's practicing an author's craft. Lifting also applies to reading, especially in standardized tests. Often students are asked to explain their thinking *using examples from the text*. I teach the kids that it's okay to embed entire lines in their answer—when a test asks for proof, pull it out!

One-to-One

I see that Bret hasn't started and needs a little more support. He's frustrated.

> **Me:** How's it going?

> **Brett:** I don't know what to write.

> **Me:** Do you want some help from me getting started? Because you have to do this.

> **Brett** [*grudgingly*]: Okay.

> **Me:** Do you have any ideas that you're trying to describe? That's the place to start.

> **Brett:** No.

> **Me:** I know how much you love baseball. Can we write about baseball? What adverbs or -*ly* words could you use to start a sentence about baseball? For example, *quickly* or *slowly* might work. You know baseball better than I do, what do you think?

> **Brett** [*thinking*]: Yeah, that makes sense. I could do pitching, huh. [*After thinking some more*] *Suddenly the pitcher on the mound wound up and threw a blazing fastball. Strike!*

> **Me:** I think you've got it! I like how you added *blazing* to the sentence for detail. I also enjoyed *Strike!* Can you do some more? You could continue with baseball or move on to something else.

> **Brett:** Yeah, I think I'm set. Thanks.

> **Me:** You're welcome. I can't wait to see what else you come up with.

Owning the Lesson

Often we look at the text as a whole to teach writing. Can you break mentor texts into smaller pieces? Some authors spend *days* crafting a single sentence. That's hard for kids to fathom. What a powerful idea—to *lift* a small section from a well-written text, analyze it, and then try to mirror the style. That truly is mentor text. Think about your own writing. How often are you asked to write a certain type of text? What do you do? You look for examples to pattern your writing on. You break it down and analyze it, then you try it yourself. How could you take this lesson and use it in your own classroom? Could the same idea be used across content areas? Is the writing students do for science structured differently? How would you model that? Technical writing?

Questions to Think About

- What is my purpose for teaching writing? How do I give my students specific examples or models, and how much are they able to practice?

- Is the practice authentic? How does it transfer to student writing?

- Can specific lines be lifted from different genres or modes to model how authors write differently for purpose and audience?

- Are my students invited to notice what authors do?

- Are my students invited to join the search for interesting sentences?

- Do my students study author's craft? Across content areas?

Writing Poetry

Introduction

If students have been immersed in poetry and quick-writes, they should have a wealth of writing in their writer's notebook. It's time to write a poem on fall (or anything else that you—or the students—choose) that will be finalized and posted in the hallway for a large audience. Think about your purpose. For example, the topic of fall still allows a lot of student choice. Or you might choose a math or social studies umbrella topic—civil rights, space exploration, urban renewal, and so on. I start with free verse, so students have a lot of leeway.

MENTOR TEXTS FOR TEACHERS

- Regie Routman's *Kids' Poems: Teaching Third and Fourth Graders to Love Writing Poetry* (2000)

MATERIALS FOR STUDENTS

- Poetry books
- Poems in reading folders
- Writer's notebook

TIME: 1 or 2 weeks, start to finish

Here's How It Goes

"You have so much writing in your notebook already, don't you? Now it's time to dig for crystals, as Ralph Fletcher calls it. We have read a lot of poems. Right now I want you to do two things. First, I want you to go back through your writing folder and find one or two poems you really enjoyed. Look for poems you might use as mentor texts, because it's your turn to write a poem; you'll draft it this week and finalize it next week. Then, I want you to go back through your writer's notebook and find pieces or lines or words that you love and might want to turn into a poem about fall."

Trinity's hand immediately shoots into the air. "I have a bunch of poems already written. Can I take parts from all of them, combine them, and turn them into a new poem?"

"What do you think? Do you think writers do that?"

"I guess so. Cool. I've already done a lot of work," says Trinity with relief.

Dexter chimes in. "What if I want to start a new poem? Something that's not in my notebook? I want to write about Halloween."

"That's fine, too," I answer. "Your only requirement is that you write a poem with phenomenal word choice."

Students ask a few more questions, then everyone gets to work. After they've gone through their folders and notebooks, I give them time to confer with a partner. This allows students to talk about their writing and clarify their ideas and receive feedback. Allowing students to talk through their thinking about their writing ahead of time solidifies their ideas and makes it easier to get the actual words down on paper (or in the computer file).

THE LANGUAGE OF LEARNING

I love to study authors. If I study and know a few authors well and can talk about their writing, then my students have the inside view. Some of my favorites are Cynthia Rylant, Avi, Gary Paulsen, Eve Bunting, Jane Yolen, Patricia Polacco, Jonathan London, and Douglas Florian. All these authors have written kid-accessible memoirs that explain how they write. And of course I love Ralph Fletcher. He writes for teachers and he also writes for children. His books *A Writer's Notebook: Unlocking the Writer Within You* (1996), *Live Writing: Breathing Life into Your Words* (1999), *Poetry Matters: Writing a Poem from the Inside Out* (2002), and *How Writers Work: Finding a Process That Works for You* (2000) all explain to students how to write authentically. The "digging for crystals" metaphor is found in Chapter 11 of *A Writer's Notebook*. It means writers dig through all their writing in their notebook (in my students' case, numerous quick-writes) to see whether there are crystals they can take out and polish to create a finished piece.

Figure 2.6 A Quick-Write in Trinity's Notebook

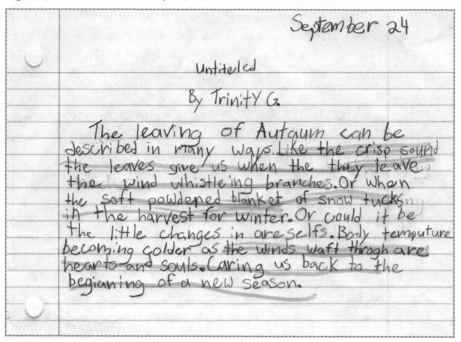

> September 24
>
> Untitled
>
> By Trinity G.
>
> The leaving of Autaum can be described in many ways. Like the crisp sound the leaves give us when the they leave. the wind whistle'ing branches. Or when the soft powdered blanket of snow tucks in the harvest for winter. Or could it be the little changes in are selfs. Body temputure becoming colder as the winds waft thragh are hearts and souls. Caring us back to the begianing of a new season.

This lesson initiates the process of crafting a poem—drafting, finalizing, and sharing with an audience. Although poetry can be written quickly, it takes time to create a well-written poem. Although students may have a wealth of "crystals" in their writer's notebook, they need to envision and plan, then draft. We spend a great deal of time conferring, revising, redrafting, often starting over. Because poetry is short, students are willing to take more risks, to attempt to write a poem in a variety of ways. They know they will make the deadline! When students have the content and form of the poem set, then we edit, finalize, and often illustrate. Because not all students finish at the same time (that's the way it is in a writing workshop), many choose to write additional poems, often on other topics. (See Figure 2.6.)

We had read a lot of poetry shaped to resemble its subject (concrete poems), and Jinu was determined to shape his poem like a leaf. It worked:

Fall
by Jinu

As fall
begins, the
leaves change like
fireworks in the black
sky. As the days pass,
more leaves dwindle down
so they can hide from the
bitterness of the winter. Until
they burst out of hiding like
groundhogs woken from
hibernation as they start
new life in the spring.
As they grow and
grow and grow
sprouting new
leaves that
will
be
sent
away
next
fall.

And here's Annie's poem:

Fall

Summer warmth has gone hibernating leaving us all
sad.
Temperatures are dropping like the rain oozing from the
clouds, leaving wet puddles of salty tears.
Instead of emerald green leaves, dazzling colors shine
through the sky.

You wake up to the morning air sending a chill through
your body.
When you walk outside you step on the grass, sopping
wet with the morning dew.
Sometimes the clouds stay as if they are trying to annoy
you.
Fall stays until that last leaf thinks it's time to let go
and the first snowflake, unlike any other, falls to the
ground with a soft thump.

Pressing Your Advantage

Reading poetry doesn't transfer to *writing* poetry. No matter how much poetry I put in front of them, most of my students draft in paragraph form. They still haven't internalized line breaks or white space. I always have to be explicit. Georgia Heard (1989) says it beautifully:

> One of the most basic units of organization of a poem, and one that affects not only how the poem looks on the page but how it sounds, is the line break. It is fundamental to a poem as a sentence or a paragraph is to a story—maybe even more so. No poem can be called finished (unless it's a prose poem) until the author has organized the poem into lines. (60)

To help students understand the importance of line breaks and white space, I ask for permission from one of my students to use one of their rough drafts to demonstrate. I put the piece on the document camera next to a piece of published poetry I've previously given the kids. Then, I ask the kids, "What do you notice about these two pieces? Just by looking at them, what's the difference?" Students typically respond something like this: "One looks like a paragraph. The poetry looks like poetry." I use this observation as a springboard to explain, "Poetry doesn't have to be sentences. The author gets to decide where to stop the lines. That's called inserting line breaks. Here's the coolest thing though—where you stop or make a line break, you're telling your reader to take a break. So you decide how you want your poem to be read." Then, I take the student example and demonstrate a variety of ways that line breaks could be used.

▶ **THE NITTY-GRITTY**

Line breaks are easy to create and play with when students are word processing. When they're writing by hand, I have them try different looks and then insert slashes in their drafts where they want the break.

Figure 2.7 Carolyn's Venn Diagram Based on Love/Hate Poems

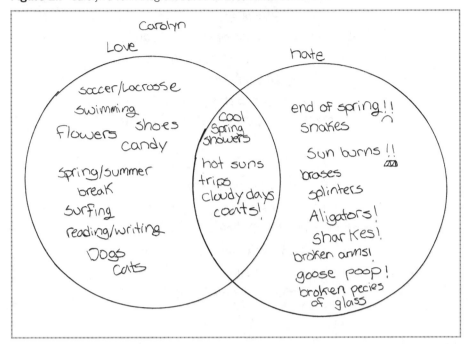

I remind kids that lines and spacing create a poem's rhythm and flow. Poetry is a kind of music, so it needs to be read aloud before being finalized. Sometimes having student authors hand their poem over to another student and listen to their peer read it with line breaks helps them decide where to leave white space.

You could also teach the entire poetry-writing lesson again through a more structured lens, perhaps having students create a Venn diagram capturing the images in two poems that compare and contrast and then write "I love" and "I hate" poems. Carolyn's Venn diagram, shown in Figure 2.7, is based on Douglas Florian's poems "What I Hate About Autumn" and "What I Love About Autumn" (both included in *Autumblings* (Greenwillow Books, 2003)). Carolyn's final poems are shown below.

▶ **THE NITTY-GRITTY**

If students are writing a specific type of poetry, the line breaks may be more formal. That would require a totally different lesson.

▶ **THE NITTY-GRITTY**

This variation on the poetry-writing lesson is also a wonderful way to teach and practice comparison/contrast writing.

What I Love About Spring

Spring brings life to everybody
Swimming and splish splashing till you faint
Flowers are blooming to see the sun

With the hot sun melting on you like butter on
Pancakes
The blue on blue skies are as bright as can be
Soccer and lacrosse games start on the green on
Green lush grass
Spring break starts!!
Birds and butterflies waft and fill the sky with
Color
Iridescent rainbows polished with glitter appear
Like coming out of hiding after rainstorms
The tree tips are shining like prisms
Dogs bark in a rythmatic sound and make me
Grow a smile and with white on white teeth shine in
The sun
The starting of spring I LOVE!!

What I HATE About Spring!!
Why does spring have to ruin everything??
Goose poop fills the grass like a green on green picnic blanket
Splinters get stuck like ticks and hurt like shots at the doctor's
Office
Burning sunburns are as red as fire and peel like yellow on yellow
Bananas
Cloudy days that cover up the sun and you feel like the world is
A giant shadow
Creeping snakes come out of nowhere and snap like
Sharks and slither up you like someone hugging
Brothers are as annoying as wasps
With the freezing cold pools you feel lucky you are in Antarctica
And shiver and shake like a Chihuahua
Bees are as loud as red on red fire trucks and ruin everything!!!!
Kids are screaming at the cool pool crying and pounding to their
Moms saying MOM!!!
Why is there always something that has to ruin spring???

Now that my students are accomplished readers and writers of poetry, I use poetry anthologies (see Davis and Hill 2003) to keep poetry in my classroom throughout the year. Each month students choose two *published* poems. These may be poems we've studied in class or poems they select themselves. (Sometimes students choose poems published—that is, revised and taken public—by students I've had in previous years. Using poems by students just like themselves as a mentor text is powerfully validating.) Kids follow their passions and interests on these poetry hunts. To keep the poetry search from dominating our workshop time, I encourage students to collect poetry at home or when they have extra time in class (another reason I have so many poetry books easily accessible). Many times, students choose poetry for their independent reading or work on their connections when they've finished other assigned work.

The first page of the poetry anthology is the title page. After that, the published poem is placed on the left page, the student's connection piece on the right.

In September students create their title page and work on their first two pages, choosing a poem and writing a connection piece. The connection piece is nothing more than a quick-write, revised, edited, and finalized; it doesn't have to be a poem. Most students choose that format, but the connection piece can be about structure or topic, even specific words. Anyone reading the two pieces must be able to understand the connection between the two.

If you look through professionally published poetry anthologies, you'll notice artwork, photographs, illustrations: There is a connection between the words and art. We need to make our classroom writing mirror the real world. Therefore, to emphasize that the anthology is a published book, I also have students illustrate or decorate the pages so that the work is beautiful. In the current rush-rush world of education with its emphasis on standards, art can be pushed aside. This slows things down a bit.

Because this is a yearlong project, it can also be an assessment. Some years each student chooses two of their favorite poems/connections, and we put them all together in a class anthology. I run off copies and bind a copy for each student. A copy also goes on the classroom poetry shelf for students in subsequent years to use as mentor texts.

When Kids Don't Get It

There are still those children who just don't know where to start. Therein lies part of the power of doing so many quick-writes and having so many mentor texts.

Kids have a scaffold—they have something to hang on to. Sometimes it just takes sitting with them and taking the time to peruse their writer's notebook to find nuggets that can be turned into poetry.

One-to-One

Ryan asks for a conference. (Getting started is tough for him, but once he gets "over the hump," he's fine. I know this is his learning style.)

Me: You asked for a conference. What can I do for you?

Ryan: I don't know how to get started. I can't do this.

Me: Let's turn that around, because you absolutely can. I've seen your quick-writes in your notebook. We'll start there. [*We start thumbing through his writing, and I pause when I see his poem about birds.*] I still really like that line about the birds flying high. I like how you used the word *gliding*.

> **THE LANGUAGE OF LEARNING**
>
> How many times has the word *wafts* shown up in these students' writing? Kids love words. And when we supply them with great vocabulary and give them opportunities to use words, we give them the power to make their writing better. *Wafts* is on an anchor chart hanging in the room, but Ryan has *heard* it as well, when other students have shared their writing. And now he wants to use it. That's another reason talk and sharing and risk taking are so essential to the writing workshop.

Ryan: I want to try a different word, like *wafting*. Lots of kids have used that and I really like it. I think that will make my poem better.

Me: Okay, great. Let's jot that here on our planning page. Can I make a suggestion? Can we take a highlighter and go through your writer's notebook and highlight words or phrases or ideas that interest you or that you think might be great in a poem? I'll get you started.

Ryan [*flipping through pages, finding a quick-write in which he has played with color words, and highlighting the words* blood red]: I just really like that.

Me: That's a start. You keep going without me, and I'll come back in a bit and check in. Anything else you need?

Ryan: Nope.

When I stop back, Ryan has started to transfer his highlighted words and phrases to his planning page. He looks up at me and says, "I don't need you right now, I've been talking with Sydney and I think I have an idea. Can I write and I'll let you know later if I need another conference?" Absolutely! Here's what he came up with (I have corrected the spelling):

Fall

Summer is dying
Fall is flying
The leaves are shedding their summer coats
To blood red skin
They leave with the wind that bites you and wafts in your way
All you want to do is get inside and play
Fall is an artist's brush from
The bristles of trees to the
Pretty colorful leaves that fall gives us
Fall is a gift.

Look at the surprises in Ryan's poetry—the visuals of the leaves shedding their summer coats to expose blood red skin and the bristles of trees becoming an artist's brush. Ryan is using specific, visual language.

Owning the Lesson

Poetry is a short form of writing that *all* students can approach successfully. How do you teach poetry in your classroom? Who makes the decisions regarding topic and form? Think about the preceding mentor texts and lessons and how everything comes together. Are there pieces or lessons you can weave together naturally in your classroom?

Questions to Think About

- What types of poetry do I need to teach in my curriculum?
- Do my students own the poetry in my classroom?
- Do my students work through the writing process?
- Are my students passionate about poetry?
- Does poetry span the year or is it a self-contained unit?
- Why do I use poetry in the classroom? (It's all about purpose!)

Wrap-Up

Facility with language gives students power in their writing. In this second lesson cluster, I weave "reading like writers" into the writing workshop using great mentor texts. The pieces students write in these lessons are short, but they lead to increased stamina and also lay the foundation for longer pieces. Surrounding students with well-written texts and then analyzing what authors do transfers into powerful student writing.

This cluster of lessons emphasizes poetry and picture books, but why stop there? Use them as a springboard to bring in a wide variety of texts for students to mirror and emulate so that they expand their vocabulary, take risks in their own writing, and *improve*. That's the bottom line, isn't it? We want to provide our students with the tools and explicit instruction they need to become better writers, to communicate effectively through written text. What better way than to put great text in front of them and ask them to practice in small, manageable doses?

What About Assessment?

I co-create checklists with my students so that they know expectations *before* beginning to write and are able to evaluate their work *after* writing. You might also design rubrics in the same way.

I use these same assessment tools to score their final pieces, offering written comments. I also use the six-traits writing rubric to score finished pieces, although I may score only a few traits at a time. For example, if we are working on beautiful language, I may score students on word choice (and also mechanics and conventions if it's a final piece, to incorporate these CCSS language standards). If it's poetry we're working on, I may use all the traits *except* sentence fluency. It's important, though, that the students know ahead of time how they are going to be evaluated. My main goal is for students to take risks and push themselves as

92

writers and then to reflect on and explicitly name what they tried, often mirroring mentor texts. I want to honor their attempts and celebrate their growth.

Throughout this cluster there are ample opportunities for students to *practice*. I emphasize again that it's *practice with a purpose*. Students are using published authors as mentors, and I'm in there *teaching*. When it's time to score a final piece, I've been interacting with each student and explicitly teaching that child something that will help him or her grow as a writer. I love Lucy Calkins's mandate, "Teach the *writer*, not the *writing*." I keep anecdotal notes on each conference with each student, which also become part of my assessment.

What Else?

Although the lessons in this cluster can stand alone, they are better when they build on one another. They are also the backbone of all future units of study throughout the year. As you read Lesson Clusters Three and Four, you'll notice that elements of these lessons reappear, so that I'm sure to give students the background knowledge they need for future work.

Often teachers who use six-traits writing in their classrooms ask which trait I start with. The six traits are a way to *evaluate* student writing, they're not a program, but I do want my students to know what each trait encompasses. So I introduce each trait and examine it, often having students create rubrics for that trait. No matter which grade I'm teaching, I love to start with word choice. I want my students noticing language and gaining power over their writing. Why not organization first? Because you've got to have vocabulary to communicate. However, organization is embedded in all the lessons in this section: Students are noticing how authors write, and that is the most authentic way to teach organization.

I sprinkle these lessons into my writing workshop throughout the year. We practice using mentor texts from August through June; mentor texts scaffold our units of study. I choose different books to do short writing projects in between units of study. We generally study three or four books a year and do a short writing project based on what we notice from the text and how the author writes.

The same goes for poetry. Poetry is present in the room year-round. I pull out poetry when I want a short text to teach specific skills: figurative language, grammar (especially strong nouns and verbs), voice, and of course making inferences.

Even better, if you find books you love and the students love, you can revisit them throughout the year. Some years I use Ralph Fletcher's *Twilight Comes*

Twice (Clarion Books, 1997) every couple of months to teach different skills. Once you start reading like a writer, you too will start to notice how you can use a favorite text to teach a variety of skills.

Things to Think About

Which lessons in this cluster jumped out at you? Prompted you to say, "I could do that" or "My students could really use that lesson"? As you read through these lessons, did certain texts immediately come to mind? Books that perhaps you've read to your students in your reading workshop but may not have used to teach writing explicitly? As you read through these lessons, did you think of a few authors that you'd like to dig into, study, bring their writing into your classroom? Ones that you could become an expert on?

Here are some other questions to think about:

- How do I teach language and vocabulary in my classroom? What do my students need to grow and improve as writers, and what aspects could I take away from these lessons and incorporate into my writing workshop?

- Who is in charge of noticing? Are all my students writing about the same things, or am I providing great texts and then letting them choose? (More and more frequently, the scorers of state writing tests comment that it's obvious when classes of students have been given a few formulaic sentences with great language to drop into their writing tests. It backfires! Instead, give kids strong vocabulary that they own and internalize, along with the knowledge to construct powerful sentences appropriate to the purpose and audience.)

- How do I teach poetry in my classroom? When? How often? With what purpose in mind?

- How can I use the concept of mentor texts to enhance writing instruction?

Writing Fictional Narratives

The previous lesson clusters, generally speaking, teach students some major truths about writing:

- It comprises beautiful, precise language.

- It's alive and quite well, thank you, in the nonfiction genres, as any trip to a bookstore will attest.

- Poetry is a "pocket-size" genre that lends itself to young writers.

In addition, they teach kids lifelong habits and skills, including:

- Note taking and paragraphing

- Quick-writes

- Using a writer's notebook

- Learning and using strong, precise vocabulary

Wonderful books, if not the stars, are key players. The picture books, poetry, and young adult literature I use as role models and the chapter books, novels, and nonfiction students dig into during independent reading and at home become part of students' language banks, their notebook entries, their identities as writers.

95

To Learn More

Independent reading is a large component of my reading workshop. For information on independent reading procedures and expectations, see Chapter 2 of *The Inside Guide to the Reading–Writing Classroom: Strategies for Extraordinary Teaching*.

In Lesson Clusters Three and Four, wonderful books take center stage in helping students explore the writing process more deeply. These mentor texts, and the lessons in which they are featured, guide students as they take their pieces to completion. They truly begin to read like writers and write like readers. They begin to notice the author's craft.

At this point in the year I begin to move away from short studies on mentor texts and their structure into longer studies focused on a genre or a topic. These *units of study* are the entire focus of Katie Wood Ray's *Study Driven* (2006). So that you can dip into this teaching without feeling you're going in too deep, this lesson cluster supports a unit of study on fiction; Lesson Cluster Four supports one on nonfiction.

Units of Study

A writing unit of study is inquiry-based. It's an immersion in a genre or topic that can take from three to six weeks and culminates with a polished piece of writing. The fiction unit I present here generally takes my students three (maximum, four) weeks to complete. The process is generally divided into the five stages Ray defines on page 19 of *Study Driven*:

- *Gathering texts*—My students and I gather examples of the kind of writing students will do.

- *Setting the stage*—I tell my students they will be expected to finish a piece of writing that shows the influence of the study.

- *Immersion*—My students and I read and get to know the texts they're studying. They make notes of things they notice about how the texts are written. They think about the *process* writers use to craft texts like the ones they are studying.

- *Close study*—We revisit the texts, framing our talk with the question, "What did we notice about how these texts are written?" Together, we state what we notice in specific language. By modeling, I help students envision how to use this learning in their own writing.

- *Writing under the influence*—Students complete pieces of writing that show the influence of the study.

When do I introduce a unit of study? When my students are ready—that is, when they understand the writing process, the expectations of the writing workshop, and how to use their writer's notebook and when they are truly noticing author's craft and beginning to use mentor texts.

▶ **THE NITTY-GRITTY**

If units of study are new to you, start small, create success, and build on that. What genres or structures do you need to teach? Poetry? Memoir? Biography? Personal narrative? Opinion pieces? Editorials? How to revise? How to use punctuation effectively? The options are many—but choose carefully!

Writing Fiction

Writing fiction is hard. Really hard. Although I am an avid reader of fiction and I understand the structure, coming up with an *idea* to write about is tough. I can write personal narrative, memoir, poetry, nonfiction, but my creative juices don't flow when it comes to fiction. You have to create believable characters, you have to have a plot (and generally conflict), and you have to hold the reader's interest. (Then, too, there are so many subgenres: realistic fiction, historical fiction, short stories, fairy tales, fantasy, and on and on.) Yet, what do our students read, and read a lot? Fiction, usually novels by the intermediate grades. And they want to write fiction, because it mirrors their reading lives.

Because this book is about mirroring reading and writing, fiction needs to be included. Although it's a difficult genre for me personally, I value teaching it, and my students are passionate about it. We take risks together, and we learn to appreciate even more the authors that craft great fiction!

Aligning Your Instruction with the Common Core State Standards

Interestingly, in many of the standards writing "mirrors" reading. The Common Core State Standards (CCSS) for writing narratives are the main focus here, but these lessons also address the reading-literature standards—students must have a deep understanding of character, setting, plot, and theme to craft fiction. And because students write a final piece, language standards are also woven into the lessons.

COLLEGE AND CAREER READINESS ANCHOR STANDARDS FOR WRITING

TEXT TYPES AND PURPOSES

1. Write narratives to develop real or imagined experiences or events using effective technique, well-chosen details, and well-structured event sequences.

Kids write narratives that include the elements of fiction: details, the sequence of events, well-created characters, dialogue, strong beginnings and leads.

PRODUCTION AND DISTRIBUTION OF WRITING

2. Produce clear and coherent writing in which the development, organization, and style are appropriate to task, purpose, and audience.

3. Develop and strengthen writing as needed by planning, revising, editing, rewriting, or trying a new approach.

4. Use technology, including the Internet, to produce and publish writing and to interact and collaborate with others.

A unit of study takes students through the entire writing process, planning to final product. Students produce and share a narrative story, and many times it is word processed.

RANGE OF WRITING

5. Write routinely over extended time frames (time for research, reflection, and revision) and shorter time frames (a single sitting or a day or two) for a range of tasks, purposes, and audiences.

Stamina, stamina, stamina! A unit of study spans a period of weeks, so students are writing routinely. There is also ample time for reflection, which is incredibly important for deepening understanding of writing and the writer's process.

COLLEGE AND CAREER READINESS ANCHOR STANDARDS FOR READING

KEY IDEAS AND DETAILS

6. Analyze how and why individuals, events, and ideas develop and interact over the course of a text.

This standard fits so beautifully with 'reading like writers'—students must read and understand fiction to write fiction or narrative.

CRAFT AND STRUCTURE

7. Analyze the structure of texts, including how specific sentences, paragraphs, and larger portions of the text (e.g., a section, chapter, scene, or stanza) relate to one another and the whole.

Once more, by reading and analyzing the craft and structure of literature, students can then write it. These books become mentor texts. In the lessons on leads and endings, students analyze mentor texts before they craft their own.

RANGE OF READING AND LEVEL OF TEXT COMPLEXITY

8. Read and comprehend complex literary and informational texts independently and proficiently.

Students need to be reading—and reading a lot—in a wide range of genres. Reading literature is the focus of 50 percent of the CCSS, so students should have at least 50 percent of their reading centered on well-written, appropriate literature. As you read through this lesson cluster, you will notice the importance of mentor texts and how students' reading informs their writing. There's certainly no better indicator of proficient reading than being able to successfully pattern writing on what has been read!

Gathering Texts and Setting the Stage

Immersion

Introduction

You'll need at least a week to read fiction, notice the format (and record these characteristics on anchor charts), read some more fiction, and start to daydream. I'll say it again: Writing fiction is hard. You not only have to write well, but you also have to come up with a story (and characters) that will hold your reader's attention. Writing fiction means taking risks, and I want my students to know that.

I allow students to choose which subgenre they want to try, because I know they will attempt to mirror the type of reading they enjoy. (I also explicitly teach that fiction is *not* retelling a movie or a TV show.) Because I stress that to be a good writer, one must read, read, read, I let them choose what they're familiar with. I see this in the first status of the class that I conduct when I ask, "What type of genre or subject within fiction are you envisioning writing about?" Some answers are:

- Dragons
- Humor
- Realistic fiction
- Fairies
- Comic books
- Picture books
- Pirates

- Sports

- Friendship

- Animals

Again, make this your own. Some teachers love to do a unit of study on writing mysteries or science fiction or realistic fiction. The key is to have a wealth of published examples so that students can immerse themselves in the format and model it authentically.

MENTOR TEXTS FOR STUDENTS

- Avi's *The Good Dog* (Simon & Schuster, 2001) and *Something Upstairs* (Scholastic, 1988)

- Lois Lowry's *All About Sam* (Houghton Mifflin, 1988)

- Ingrid Law's *Savvy* (Penguin, 2008)

- Jacqueline Woodson's *Locomotion* (Penguin, 2003) and *Peace, Locomotion* (Penguin, 2009)

- Sharon Creech's *Love That Dog* (HarperCollins, 2001) and *Hate That Cat* (HarperCollins, 2008)

- Paul Fleischman's *The Half-a-Moon Inn* (HarperCollins, 1980)

- Frank Cottrell Boyce's *Cosmic* (HarperCollins, 2010)

- N. D. Wilson's *100 Cupboards* (Random House, 2007)

- Emily Rodda's *Deltora Quest* (Scholastic, 2000)

- Marion Dane Bauer's *On My Honor* (Houghton Mifflin, 1986)

- Kate DiCamillo's *Because of Winn-Dixie* (Candlewick, 2000)

- Gary Paulsen's *How Angel Peterson Got His Name* (Random House, 2003)

- Rick Riordan's *The Lightning Thief* (Hyperion, 2005)

- Jeff Kinney's *Diary of a Wimpy Kid* (Abrams, 2007)

- Louis Sachar's *Holes* (Farrar, Straus and Giroux, 1998)

- Patricia Reilly Giff's *Pictures of Hollis Woods* (Random House, 2002)

▶ **THE NITTY-GRITTY**

This list no doubt makes you think of some of the students you've had, the ones who want to cut corners or take the easy way out. They may jump at the chance to write a picture book. However, if you break down the *amount* of text included in a picture book—at least a couple of typed pages—that's the same as a short story. And picture books need a plot and in some ways a tighter control of language. Think of the beautifully written picture books you bring in to share, full of rich, specific language. Students who choose that option still need to mirror a mentor text, and they have to write exceedingly well. There's no easy way out!

- Appropriate short stories and picture books (these shorter, more manageable texts are important and useful, but I'm saving space and not listing individual titles)

MATERIALS FOR STUDENTS

- Fiction in a wide variety of reading levels, lengths, and genres
- Writer's notebook

TIME: 30 minutes

▶ **THE NITTY-GRITTY**

New fiction is released at such a fast clip, it's often hard to keep up. In my periodic treks to the bookstore, I'm overwhelmed by how many new releases there are. I encourage you to stay up-to-date with quality literature. And of course watch what the students bring in—they're the best indicators of what is popular and informing their writing!

Here's How It Goes

"I promised we'd do a unit of study on writing fiction. You've already given me a list of some of the genres you read and like. Today, I'd like you to start a list in your writer's notebook of titles or topics or anything else that you'd like to write a fictional story about. Just start brainstorming. This list can keep growing as you think of ideas to add to it. You might like to think about books or topics you enjoy and piggyback off them. And you might start looking for mentor texts. If you find a book that you think would help you write, bring it in. We're going to spend this week just brainstorming and talking about what makes good fiction. Let's work on those lists for about fifteen minutes, then I'd like you to share some of your ideas in groups of four."

▶ **THE NITTY-GRITTY**

Some students (we all have them!) are going to say they don't enjoy any fiction or don't have any ideas. This is a great opportunity to pull a group together to brainstorm. I have them bring their book lover's book (BLB) list of books they've read. I also point out our Reading to 100 list (every time I read a book for a minilesson or we complete a read-aloud, we add it to a wall chart—concrete evidence of all our shared reading in a wide variety of genres). Then we look at our lists and discuss which genres each of us likes. As we brainstorm, students record their ideas in their writer's notebook.

Pressing Your Advantage

How often do you come up with a topic—especially for fiction—in a thirty-minute brainstorming session? It's the same with kids. During this week of immersing ourselves in text, I spend part of every writing workshop reading a new piece of text in connection with a minilesson and adding characteristics to our class chart of what makes good fiction. Students are pretty adept at identifying the elements of good fiction, but I push them to explain or expand their answers and their thinking. They pick up on setting and plot, characters and dialogue, and most important, how essential it is to hold your reader's attention.

In addition to my reading fiction and narratives to them, the students also find and share examples of great fiction. We end up with a large assortment of fiction representative of all the students and all their interests. During this time students identify a mentor text they will use as a model or springboard for their own writing. I also encourage the kids to start "daydreaming"—creating their stories. Fiction needs a lot of planning.

▶ **THE NITTY-GRITTY**

Testing is a reality for all of us. I want my students to do well, to get high scores. However, I also want to continue to teach authentically. During this period of immersion, I use each day's minilesson to explicitly teach a specific element or skill. For example, I might read Scott Russell Saunders' *Crawdad Creek* (National Geographic Children's, 2002) in connection with teaching students about *setting*. If my focus is *cause and effect*, I might read Mark Teague's *Detective LaRue: Letters from the Investigation* (Scholastic, 2004) and either model creating a cause-and-effect chart based on the book or ask the students to construct one independently. Look at the skills that are part of your curriculum or required in your students' standardized tests and think about how you could embed them here.

When Kids Don't Get It

Mostly what the kids don't get is what to write about, especially because I've told them that retelling movies or video games is off limits. Kids who don't like to read or aren't voracious readers can get stuck. Kids who watch a ton of TV want to write TV shows. This is a great time to discuss how even movies and TV shows (and video games for that matter) require scripts. That sometimes can segue into an idea.

If they're still stuck, it's imperative that I know the kids as people. What are their passions? What are they good at? How can their interests turn into a story? Because realistic fiction is an available subgenre, I give them the option of writing about something they know well, as long as they create fictional characters.

One-to-One

It can be difficult to make up our mind—we may need a little guidance or maybe another point of view. Lucie has been talking with friends about possible stories and even drawing maps and sketching characters, but she finally asks for a conference.

Lucie: Okay, I'm stuck. I can't make up my mind if I want to write about these two hamsters that get stuck in Candy Land and eat their way through everything, or if I want to write a story about two friends who get in a fight. I don't know which would be better.

Me: Wow, those are two totally different types of stories. Which one do you like better?

Lucie: I don't know. I loved Candy Land as a kid and I think it would be fun to write about, but I don't know how I'll do writing a fantasy.

Me: How about the other?

Lucie: That might be easier, because I know that friends get in fights all the time. I'd just need to figure out something good that they'd be fighting about.

Me: Sounds as if you've thought about both. Are you worried that the Candy Land story might be risky?

Lucie: Kind of, yeah. Like what if I start and I don't like where I'm going?

Me: Don't you think that happens to authors all the time? What do you think they do?

Lucie: They start over? Can they change their minds?

Me: Of course! That's the beauty of writing. Time and choice and change. You can't do that when you talk, can you? You can't take your words back. So what do you think I'm going to tell you as your writing teacher?

Lucie: To try Candy Land?

Me: No, I'm going to tell you to choose the one you're more interested in writing. Because if you get bored as the writer, your reader got bored two pages earlier. Take a risk. Try something new—that's what writing workshop is for. And we have time, so you can change your mind. Does that help?

Lucie: So, you meant it when you said our reflections and what we tried were going to be a big part of our evaluation?

Me: Yes. Fiction is tough. I want you taking risks and trying new things and then *reflecting* about that and how you *changed* as a writer. If we always go with what's safe, we never get better. Anything else you need?

Lucie: No, not now. But I'll need more conferences when I'm drafting.

Me: I can't wait!

Owning the Lesson

For a week—at least a week, it could be more—students immerse themselves in narrative and fiction before beginning to draft. In our hurry-up world, a week could seem a luxury. But in the long run, if we give our students a strong foundation before they begin drafting, the writing goes much faster. Think about all your students who are blocked or have nothing to write about or who start, abandon, and start again. Do you anticipate and address the issues that usually stand in the way of successfully finishing a writing piece? If so, this is a week well spent.

What aspects of this lesson could you pull out for either your writing or your reading instruction? For other genres? How often do you invite students on the search for well-written text? And then let them share their insights? Who does the majority of the work?

Questions to Think About

- How much time do my students usually receive to brainstorm, plan, and envision before starting to draft a narrative (or any other genre, for that matter)?

- Are my students exposed to a wide variety of well-written texts before they begin to write?

- Who chooses the topic, format, and so on?

- Do my students know how to use mentor texts to inform their own writing?

- How can I incorporate skills and concepts into a unit of study?

- How can this unit of study inform other writing in my class?

Envisioning Stories

Introduction

Once the kids know that they will be writing a fiction piece, they want to know how long it needs to be. Think about it—students generally read *novels*, and who can write a novel in three to five weeks? So we discuss the option of writing a single chapter of a book or perhaps a short story. This is my opportunity to bring in examples of short stories. I read them aloud and put them in student's hands.

We also discuss the elements of fiction:

- Characters
- Setting
- Plot (conflict or problem, climax, resolution)
- Story arc (beginning, middle, end)

Kids probably think plot is most important. But think about yourself as a reader. Which books stick with you? Which ones are unforgettable? I'm betting they're the ones with memorable *characters* or relationships between characters. Before they can create characters, students need to decide on a genre and envision how their fiction piece will look when they're done.

MENTOR TEXTS FOR STUDENTS

In addition to the ones listed in lesson 9 here are a few more:

- Georgia Byng's *Molly Moon's Incredible Book of Hypnotism* (HarperCollins, 2002)

- Wilson Rawls' *Summer of the Monkeys* (Doubleday, 1976)
- Mike Lupica's *The Big Field* (Penguin, 2008)
- Lincoln Pierce's *Big Nate: In a Class by Himself* (HarperCollins, 2010)
- Roland Smith's *Elephant Run* (Hyperion, 2007)
- Sarah Weeks's *So B. It* (HarperCollins, 2004)

MATERIALS FOR STUDENTS

- Mentor text
- Writer's notebook

TIME: 30 minutes

Here's How It Goes

"You've spent the last week thinking about your fiction pieces. You've made lists, read, noticed how authors craft fiction, and started thinking about how your piece might look. Today I want you to write me what you're thinking. What's your plan? Tell me what genre you want to write and what your mentor text will be. Are you planning to write a short story or a couple of chapters? A picture book or a graphic novel? Will you have illustrations or just text? Before we start, we need to *envision* what our end product is going to look like."

On a sheet of chart paper I write:

- Genre?
- Mentor text?
- What will it look like? Short story? Couple of chapters? Picture book? Graphic novel? Something else?
- Anything else to help me see what you're planning.

"Okay, what questions do you have?"

Lucie raises her hand. "What if we decide to change things once we start? What if our writing doesn't match our plan as we get going?"

▶ THE NITTY-GRITTY

Again you may be thinking, "My kids would choose to write a chapter because it's the easy way out." But what I said earlier about picture books is true here too: Writing a chapter takes tight control. If students choose this option, they need to analyze well-written chapters. If it's the beginning chapter, the characters, setting, and problem are introduced. The reader's attention has to be grabbed, and the chapter has to end with a hook. In many books, each chapter introduces and solves small problems, in which case the author needs to know the overall plot. My students often write two or more chapters because they are so engrossed. And the remaining chapters can become backup work—the piece they can return to when they have time. I even have students who work on these pieces over a period of years!

"What do you think? As we've been studying authors, we've discovered that sometimes the act of writing surprises authors and they make changes as they go. Do you think that will be okay here? If it makes your writing better or if it makes you a better writer, is that okay?"

The kids nod.

"Okay, let's see what you come up with. Remember, this is just the beginning. Our pieces will grow and change as we draft."

The kids go back and write for fifteen or twenty minutes, pushing themselves to extend their thinking. (See Figure 3.1.)

Figure 3.1 A Student's Handwritten Plan of a Part of His Thinking

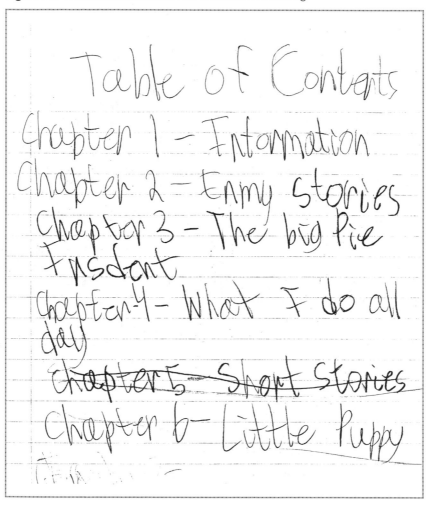

Pressing Your Advantage

I collect their envisioning plans and read them in preparation for conferring with the students and guiding their writing. I determine who is ready to go and who may need some more support and direct instruction in needs-based groups. I also make sure I have the appropriate fiction and mentor texts available. For example, if I have a lot of kids writing fantasy, I need a wide variety of fantasy books at a wide range of levels for them to turn to as they write.

When Kids Don't Get It

The kids' envisioning plans let me know which children don't have a plan or even an idea where to begin. I pull some books with similar genres and topics and work with them in a small group or individually, a mentor text at my fingertips.

One-to-One

Rachael doesn't like to read and avoids writing, and spelling is tough for her. But she has responded well to my mentor text lessons (see Cluster Two) and is a master at using authors to guide her writing. She especially loves poetry, and Cynthia Rylant is one of her favorite poets. However, writing fiction is out of her comfort zone.

Rachael: Mrs. B, I love poetry. I don't want to write fiction. Please can I just write poetry? I'm good at it.

Me: I agree, kiddo, you are. But if that's all you write, you won't grow. We grow as writers by taking risks.

Rachael: So what do I do? My favorite book is *Hatchet*, and I can't write like Paulsen, I can't write *Hatchet*.

Me: I think that's wise. Paulsen had to research, and he also had the background he needed to write that book. He lived so much of it. I think that's why we love it so much—because it's so different from the lives we live. Such a powerful book. That turned you into a reader, didn't it?

Rachael: I loved it, and I loved discussing it with my book club. And I like the beautiful language in picture books. I like to write like that. But those really aren't fiction or problem books.

Me: I get what you're saying. And I'm so happy you're finally finding books you love. You're not a big fantasy reader, so let's think of things you do love, things you know about.

Rachael: Okay, I love soccer and I love animals. I love dogs.

Me: Ever read any books about either of those topics?

Rachael: I know Matt Christopher and Mike Lupica write sports stories, but I don't want to do those. Could I do dogs?

Me: Think about dog stories you've read or heard. Any catch your interest?

Rachael: You've read a lot to us. And I love Marley stories. Could I do funny stories about my dog?

Me: What do you think? Should we go pull some Marley books and some of the other books I've read aloud and you can see whether you can find a mentor text?

Rachael: Yes.

We go find a pile of books and Rachael spends the rest of the workshop reading and thinking. She finally decides to do a picture book about a puppy that gets in constant trouble—based on her dog, of course! Put the books in the kids' hands!

Owning the Lesson

Think about your previous writing assignments. Have you asked your students to reflect and explain their plan *before* beginning to write? Or do they just dive in? What does asking students to write about their plan ahead of time do to solidify their thinking? To guide your instruction?

Does this mean students can't change their mind? Absolutely not. Writers are constantly changing their minds or taking their writing in different directions. Often the act of writing is a surprise even for the author! But having a plan—and being able to refer to that plan—helps students evaluate both the process and the final product.

What could you take away from this lesson and apply in your classroom? Even if you're not presenting units of study, are there elements of this lesson you could incorporate into your writing workshop?

Questions to Think About

- How do my students record their plan and their purpose for writing?

- Are my students expected to explain what they are writing, identify a mentor text, and state what they want to try as writers? Do I encourage them to take risks and stretch themselves as writers?

- Who is in charge of determining what students write?

- Who chooses and owns the writing?

- Are my students deliberate and purposeful about their writing? How does this inform my instruction for the whole class? For individuals?

- How could I use this lesson to improve conferences?

- How could I use this lesson to evaluate students, both their process and their product?

Creating Characters

Introduction

Because character is so important, I spend several minilessons helping students develop strong characters. Characters need names—first *and* last names. I keep phone books (white pages) and baby name books in the writing center. We also need to know our characters physically and emotionally. What makes the characters tick? It takes time to create believable characters the reader cares about. Because I want students to work on this authentically, we start by brainstorming, listing, and webbing. In follow-up lessons I give students handouts identifying things they can do to flesh out their characters.

MENTOR TEXTS FOR TEACHERS

- Barry Lane's *Reviser's Toolbox* (1999), written in response to teacher requests for blackline masters to help with revision, includes highly motivating ideas for helping students understand characters in literature and then create their own.

MENTOR TEXTS FOR STUDENTS

- Gary Paulsen's *Hatchet* (Simon & Schuster, 1987), *How Angel Peterson Got His Name* (Random House, 2003), and *Canyons* (Bantam Dell Doubleday, 1990)
- Ingrid Law's *Savvy* (Dial Books/Walden Media, 2008)
- Avi's *The True Confessions of Charlotte Doyle* (Orchard Books, 1990) and other books

- Roald Dahl's *The BFG* (Farrar, Straus and Giroux, 1982) and *Matilda* (Viking Kestrel, 1988)

- Wilson Rawls' *Where the Red Fern Grows* (Doubleday, 1961) and *Summer of the Monkeys* (Doubleday, 1976)

- Madeline L'Engle's *A Wrinkle in Time* (Farrar, Straus and Giroux, 1962)

- Pam Muñoz Ryan's *Esperanza Rising* (Scholastic, 2000)

- Will Hobbs' *Bearstone* (Simon & Schuster, 1989)

- Jeff Kinney's *Diary of a Wimpy Kid* series

- Scott O'Dell's *Island of the Blue Dolphins* (Houghton Mifflin, 1960)

- Karen Hesse's *The Music of Dolphins* (Scholastic, 1996)

- Kate DiCamillo's *The Tiger Rising* (Candlewick, 2001) and *The Tale of Desperaux* (Candlewick, 2003)

- Christopher Paul Curtis's *Bud, Not Buddy* (Random House, 1999)

- Paul Fleischman's *The Half-a-Moon Inn* (HarperCollins, 1980)

MATERIALS FOR STUDENTS

- Writer's notebook

- Mentor text

- White pages of the phone book

- Baby name books

TIME: 30 to 45 minutes over two to three days

Here's How It Goes

"Think about your favorite books. Why do you remember them?"

Kids reflect and begin to answer. Inevitably it comes down to characters. It's Big Dan and Little Ann from *Where the Red Fern Grows* and their relationship to their owner. It's Karana from *Island of the Blue Dolphins* and her will to survive and her ability to forgive. Or Brian in *Hatchet*. I tell kids you can have the best plot in the world, but if your reader doesn't care about the character, the book's a dud. And good characters have a flaw. Something they have to overcome. Flaws make us interesting. This leads to a discussion about characters in the books we are reading and their flaws. Sometime I have a few

THE LANGUAGE OF LEARNING

This lesson could also be taught during reading workshop. After independent reading, student pairs could discuss character flaws they encountered in their reading that day.

students share while we all listen. Sometimes I have students turn and talk to each other so that every voice can be heard. Or we might discuss characters in books I've read aloud to the class as anchor texts. Whatever the technique, I keep this discussion to ten minutes.

"You've been planning your piece and how it will look. Now we're going to zoom in on characters. I had a friend who wrote novels. I asked her how she did it, and she said that when she was a girl she made up a character. The character was a girl who had some of Elaine's characteristics but also a lot of attributes Elaine wished she had. Every night as she went to sleep, Elaine would create another episode in an ongoing story about this character."

Qmarah gasps, "I do that. I didn't think anyone else did that!"

"As Elaine grew up, the character grew too, and Elaine created different stories for her. When she was an adult she decided to write a real story. She knew her character so well by that point. I tell this story because authors know their characters incredibly well. You might not write everything about them, but you still know them. What they like and dislike, how they feel. Some authors say that when they write it's like the character is sitting on their shoulder helping them write.

"So we're going to begin work on our main characters today. This is your chance to brainstorm. I don't care whether you list or web or draw a sketch. The phone books and the baby name books are in the writing center if you need help with a name. I want you to work on this independently today and then tomorrow we'll share, and the day after that you'll do an interview with a partner. One of you will be the interviewer and one of you will act like your character. The interviewer will ask questions, the person being interviewed has to answer as her or his character. Then you'll switch. One other thing, though. I'm going to ask that you don't use names of kids in our class, even if you have permission. You might write something that inadvertently hurts someone's feelings. One year I had a student who used some of the kids' names but not everyone's, and that hurt too. There are so many names; I don't think this will be a big deal."

Students begin to work at their desks.

THE LANGUAGE OF LEARNING

In this lesson you can introduce/reinforce the literary terms *protagonist, antagonist, main characters, supporting characters, point of view (first person, second person, third person, third-person omniscient)*.

THE LANGUAGE OF LEARNING

Character or plot, which should be emphasized? I put character front and center in this lesson, but published authors say it depends on the writer. Think about books you read and enjoy. Does that enjoyment stem from character development or the plot? This is almost a gender issue. For *most* boys it's the plot—the action. They want action on every page. For *many girls* it's the characters and their relationships. That's why we need to teach both and value the direction the individual student takes. Even students who tend to gravitate toward plot need to think about how the characters in their piece participate in the action. Lesson 14 focuses on plot, and the lessons in this cluster do not need to be taught sequentially. If your students are ready for plot, teach it earlier in the sequence.

Pressing Your Advantage

After we brainstorm, we conduct character interviews, which helps kids solidify their thinking (and is also a lot of fun, a plus). I model the procedure with a student volunteer. I pretend to be a television reporter and ask the student questions—name, age, family, likes, dislikes, and so on. The student answers in character. Then partners interview each other—or rather the character each partner has created.

CCSS, GRADE BY GRADE

Third graders need to be able to describe the main characters in a story they are reading or using as a mentor text—in particular, their traits, motivations, and feelings. This can segue into writing in which they establish characters and describe characters' actions, thoughts, and feelings.

Fourth graders are also required to describe characters in their reading, but in *detail* and by means of a character's thoughts, words, deeds, or interactions with others. In their writing, they are expected to introduce a narrator and/or characters and show external behaviors and internal responses to events—to know the character inside and out!

Fifth graders need to be able to compare and contrast two or more characters on the basis of specific details. Students build on this knowledge as they introduce a narrator and/or characters in their writing.

Sixth graders are expected to describe how characters in their reading adapt or change as they move toward a resolution. In their writing they should convey characters' experiences with the help of precise words, descriptive details, and sensory language.

When Kids Don't Get It

It's obvious as I eavesdrop on the interviews who has a fully developed character and who has only a limited understanding of the character. I work with the latter students individually and make sure they have ample opportunities to talk about their stories.

One-to-One

Robert hasn't thoroughly thought out his character. As we talk, I write down his thoughts, so that when I leave he will have these notes to refer back to. (Robert's conferences will be featured in some of the fiction lessons that follow.)

Me: Robert, I'm not going to interview you as your character right now, but can I ask you some questions about him?

Robert: Yes.

Me: Before I ask, can you describe him to me? Tell me as much as you know.

Robert: He's a teenager and he gets in trouble and he finds a dragon and saves the town.

Me: Okay, you're planning the problem and what's going to happen in the story. He's a teenager, but what's his name?

Robert: Mac.

Me: Can you tell me the rest of his name?

Robert: I don't have that.

Me: That's one thing we need to work on. When I leave, maybe you can get the phone book and come up with his whole name. Now, what does Mac look like?

Robert: He's a teenager.

Me: How old?

Robert: Sixteen, I guess.

Me: Let me push you a little. Try to picture or visualize Mac in your mind. How tall is he? What color hair? What color skin? Does he like to smile a lot or is he serious? Is he skinny or heavy or buff? Let's start there. Think of sixteen-year-old boys you know and see whether you can use some of the things you know about them. I'm going to write a web really fast and write Mac in the middle. Then I'm going to create bubbles labeled *height, hair, weight, skin, face,* and I want you to fill those in and add a few more bubbles. Can we start there?

Robert: I'll try.

Remember, deal with only one thing in a conference. Here I start with physical characteristics. Next time we'll work on why Mac gets into trouble.

▶ **THE NITTY-GRITTY**

I'm not a huge proponent of programs loaded with graphic organizers, but they're helpful *as long as kids choose the organizer and create it themselves* (no copying one form for the entire class). I've found the visual teaching tools available through Thinking Maps Incorporated (thinkingmaps.com), which span grades K–12, a great addition to my classroom.

Owning the Lesson

When you read, do you like characters or plot more? How about when you write? Be aware of yourself as a reader and writer and share those insights with your students. Do you draw attention to character as you read aloud to your students? Or do you focus more on the plot and the problems and ultimately the resolution?

What aspects from this lesson could you apply to your writing workshop? What could you lift for your reading workshop? How is character—and knowledge of character—assessed on standardized reading and writing tests, in your curriculum, and in the standards?

Questions to Think About

- How do my students create characters?
- Do my students create believable characters? Do they know the difference between flat and round characters?
- Do my students understand the terms *protagonist* and *antagonist*?
- Do my students have access to resources that will help them create characters?
- Do my students understand the connection between reading about characters and writing characters?
- Do I emphasize characters—their development, traits, and flaws—in reading workshop?
- Do my students understand that they can live with their characters? That they can continue to create a character anytime?
- Do my students know that they can observe and notice traits of people around them and incorporate characters with these traits in the pieces they write?

Lesson 13

Sketching the Setting

Introduction

In *Boy Writers: Reclaiming Their Voices* (2006), Ralph Fletcher writes that drawing maps often helps boys organize their thoughts. Why just boys? You've probably read books that have maps at the beginning (Tolkien's *The Hobbit* and Cornelia Funke's *Dragon Rider* jump to mind). When I read *The Hobbit*, being able to refer to the map was a big help.

In realistic fiction, setting isn't as difficult to write. However, if students are writing fantasy or historical fiction, they need time to research and visualize. Giving students the opportunity to draw the topography of their setting can facilitate planning. (But I don't allow this to stretch beyond a single class period. Some of my students would spend the entire unit of study drawing! They can finish at home it they wish.)

MENTOR TEXTS FOR STUDENTS

- Avi's *Something Upstairs* (Scholastic, 1988) and *Poppy* (HarperCollins, 1995)
- Cornelia Funke's *Dragon Rider* (Scholastic, 2004)
- Will Hobbs' *Bearstone* (Simon & Schuster, 1989) and *Beardance* (Simon & Schuster, 1993)
- Norton Juster's *The Phantom Tollbooth* (Random House, 1961)
- Scott O'Dell's *Island of the Blue Dolphins* (Houghton Mifflin, 1960)
- Mary Pope Osborne's Magic Tree House series

- Gary Paulsen's *Hatchet* (Simon & Schuster, 1987)
- Pam Muñoz Ryan's *Esperanza Rising* (Scholastic, 2000)
- Louis Sachar's *Holes* (Farrar, Straus and Giroux, 1998)
- J. R. R. Tolkien's *The Hobbit* (Houghton Mifflin, 1938)
- N. D. Wilson's *100 Cupboards* (Random House, 2007)

MATERIALS FOR STUDENTS

- Examples of fiction books that include maps (invite kids on the search)
- Mentor text
- Writer's notebook
- Drawing paper

TIME: 30 to 60 minutes (no more than one class period)

Here's How It Goes

"Now that you have your character, where are you going to put him? Does your story take place in the past, the present, or the future? Turn to the person next to you and share your answer to those two questions."

Kids turn and share. As they wrap up, I ask, "How many stories take place in the past?" Kids raise their hands. "How about the present? The future? If you're writing about the past, then you might have to research what it was like during that time period. If it's the future, you might have to create it.

"Now, how about the where? How many know your setting well?" Kids raise their hands. "You might not have to spend as much time thinking about your setting as kids who are writing fantasy, but you still need to be able to visualize where and when your story is taking place. You know how much I love studying Ralph Fletcher and how he writes and what he suggests for kids. He encourages teachers to let kids sketch and draw the setting. So today that's what you can do if you want.

"Let's take a look at a couple of books with maps in them." I pull out *Beardance*, by Will Hobbs, and *Dragon Rider*, by Cornelia Funke. "I'm not saying you have to include a map in your piece, but I know as a reader I love to refer to it as I read. As a writer, sometimes having a map helps you know where your character is. For example, Lucie, you're doing Candy Land and your hamsters are going to be going all over. If you have a map, that might help you keep everything straight. If you don't want to draw, you're welcome to list, read, or start working on your writing."

In Figure 3.2 Kate has drawn the house where the hamster in her story lives (and escapes from). She knows it's important to refer to this map as her character roams around the house and outside.

Pressing Your Advantage

To tie this to reading workshop, I have students write a paragraph describing the setting of the book they are reading independently or as a member of a book club. I encourage them to critique the author's depiction of the setting. This is great practice for some standardized test questions.

When Kids Don't Get It

Students who aren't able to create a setting tend to be the same ones who are struggling with reading. As we work in a small group, I ask these students to sketch the setting of the book or piece that we are reading together. Often this entails having students talk about the setting and what they're envisioning as I take quick notes. Then I read those notes back to the students. This often helps them to clarify their ideas enough to sketch them out. Another great strategy is to head to the computer and pull up pictures and photos of places like the ones kids are envisioning. Let them see it and then turn around and sketch it.

One-to-One

Once again I check in with Robert.

> **Me:** Thanks for working so hard on your character. We've talked about how he gets into a lot of trouble in the town and goes and hides in the forest and finds the dragon and that this takes place a long, long time ago.
>
> **Robert:** And then he and the dragon save the town when the bad guys come.
>
> **Me:** So this is a fantasy. What does the town look like?
>
> **Robert:** A town. You know houses, buildings. [*I realize Robert sees a town of today, not a fantasy town of long ago with dragons.*] Tell you what. Remember how we've talked about background knowledge? Have you read many dragon books or seen

Figure 3.2 Kate's Drawing of the Setting of Her Story

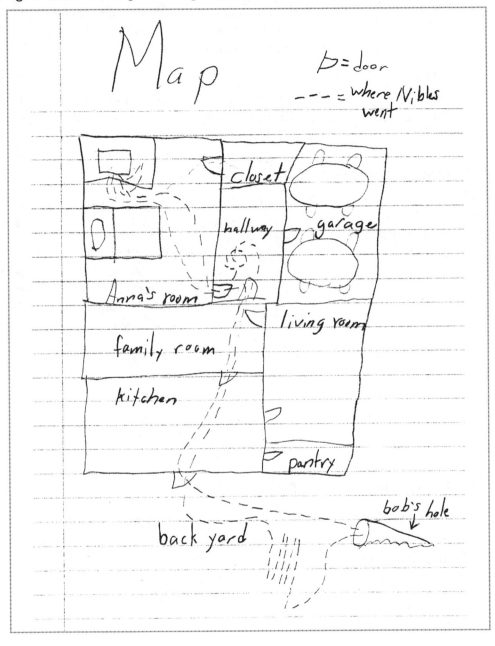

movies with dragons in them? [*Robert shakes his head*.] Then we need to go get some more mentor texts. We could look up dragons on the computer, but I think you might get better pictures if we got some books. I've got a ton in the classroom. Do you want to start with those or go to the library?

Robert: Can I go to the library?

Me: Sure, look at a lot of pictures! Maybe put sticky notes on the pages with pictures that help you envision the town and the place where your story is going to take place.

Owning the Lesson

Kids brainstorm, prewrite, and rehearse in different ways. Perhaps that's why writing is so difficult to teach—there's no one right way to do it and it's often not sequential. As you think about your students who need time to visualize or who have different learning styles, how does this lesson fit? How does it relate to boys and girls and their different approaches to literacy? Can you use this lesson not only for settings in narratives and fiction but in connection with reading and writing other genres? We want our students to write well enough for the reader to visualize—to create sensory images. How do we ensure that our students picture these images in their mind?

> **THE LANGUAGE OF LEARNING**
>
> We could take this one step further and use maps in connection with historical fiction or even social studies. When authors are writing historical fiction, the setting, the location, must be accurate. That's why authors often have to do research. Accuracy is key.

Questions to Think About

- How would sketching or drawing help my students visualize?
- How long should I let students draw or sketch? How much class time should I allot?
- Do I have books in my classroom that include maps?
- How much experience do my students have with maps? Could I integrate this lesson across the curriculum?
- What will my students do with the sketches when they finish them? Include them in their writing, or just use them as a plan?
- Do all my students need to sketch? What about those who don't want to or need to?

Plotting Promising Problems

Introduction

In reading workshop, my students and I focus on the problems or plot in the books we are reading. We examine the beginning, the middle, and the end. We look for *conflict*. I ask students to transfer these same skills to their writing.

Don Graves discusses plot in *Experiment with Fiction* (1989): "Plot is at the heart of fiction. Children seem to sense this, since they immediately focus on action in their writing. Often their problem is that action, the beginning of the plot, is everything" (27). Although I ask my students to begin with character, they're thinking plot at the same time: What's going to happen? What is the problem? How is it going to be solved? What will be the sequence? How will the characters act/react to the action of the plot?

MENTOR TEXTS FOR STUDENTS

Boys more often focus on plot. Here are some great boy-friendly books:

- Rick Riordan series
- Young James Bond series
- Any books by Mike Lupica
- Sports books
- Diary of a Wimpy Kid series
- Betty Miles' *The Secret Life of the Underwear Champ* (Knopf, 1981)
- J. K. Rowling's Harry Potter series
- Judy Blume's *Tales of a Fourth Grade Nothing* (Dutton, 1972)

MATERIALS FOR STUDENTS

- Books, books, books
- Writer's notebook
- Graphic organizers for planning the beginning, middle, and end

TIME: 45 minutes

Here's How It Goes

"We've looked at plot and problem a lot in our reading. Now it's your turn to come up with a plot. Fiction stories have some type of conflict. I'm betting you already know what the problem is going to be in your story. You've been envisioning it, working on the character, creating a setting, now we have to have the problem. This is what keeps the reader reading on. Take a few minutes right now and just think about the problem for your story." I give the kids a couple minutes to think.

"When I call your name for our status check today, give me a one-sentence description of your problem. I think everyone in the class would like to hear it." As I record their answers, I clarify as needed.

"Okay, this is it. Tomorrow we start writing, so today is our last day of planning and brainstorming. Please form compass groups and take about fifteen minutes to talk about your fiction pieces and the problem for your character. This is your opportunity to set your thinking so you'll be ready to go."

Pressing Your Advantage

Although I'm not a big proponent of worksheets, graphic organizers can help students who need help plotting the problems in their stories. At this point I often introduce plot diagrams or storyboards. For a storyboard, students draw/sketch the important pieces of the plot on note cards and arrange them on a large sheet of paper, moving the cards around to get the sequence right.

TO LEARN MORE

Chapter 7 of *The Inside Guide to the Reading–Writing Classroom* discusses the status of the class form in detail. Here's the gist. I keep a form on my clipboard with every child's name next to space to record comments (the same form for reading workshop and writing workshop, just color-coded). I use one form each week, then archive it in a three-ring binder. It's my way of documenting informal observations and holding the students and myself accountable. At the beginning of each writing workshop, I go down the list of names, and students tell me where they are in the process or what they're working on or if they need a conference with me. The students have to think about how they're going to use their workshop time—it gives them ownership. I get through twenty-five students in less than five minutes, and we all know what we're working on!

Don't want to get that elaborate? Sticky notes are also a great way to indicate a plot sequence. Figure 3.3 is Ellie's graphic representation of her plan. Figure 3.4 is an example of a storyboard.

When Kids Don't Get It

As students share their problems for status of the class, I identify students who would benefit from some more direct instruction. Later I invite these students to work with me in a group using a form such as Barry Lane's Set-Up, Mix-Up, and Fix-Up, which gives them a scaffold for their thinking. The setup is the beginning or introduction to the story, the mix-up is the problem, and the fix-up is the resolution.

One-to-One

I check in with Robert.

> **Robert** [*pointing to the Set-Up, Mix-Up, Fix-Up sheet*]: I still don't get how this fits with my story.
>
> **Me:** Barry Lane is trying to help us plan out the story—the beginning, middle, and end. The setup is how you're going to introduce the character and the problem. Why don't you tell me your thinking and I'll record it here. How do you want to start?
>
> **Robert:** Mac is in school, and he gets into trouble so he runs away and goes to the forest.
>
> **Me:** Do you want to add how he gets in trouble?
>
> **Robert:** He's a bully.
>
> **Me:** That's a start. That could almost be the problem.
>
> **Robert:** No, being a bully isn't the problem. The bad guys are.
>
> **Me:** So is that the mix-up?
>
> **Robert:** Yeah. While Mac is in the forest he meets the dragon and he learns not to be a bully. And then the bad guys are coming to burn down the town.
>
> **Me:** Okay, got it. How does it end?
>
> **Robert:** Mac wants to apologize to the school 'cause he's not a bully anymore so he and the dragon fly out and scare the bad guys away.
>
> **Me:** You've done some thinking, Robert. Now when it's time to write tomorrow, you can pull this out and see where to start and where to go with your story.

Figure 3.3 Ellie has included plot and genre and characters and even point of view.

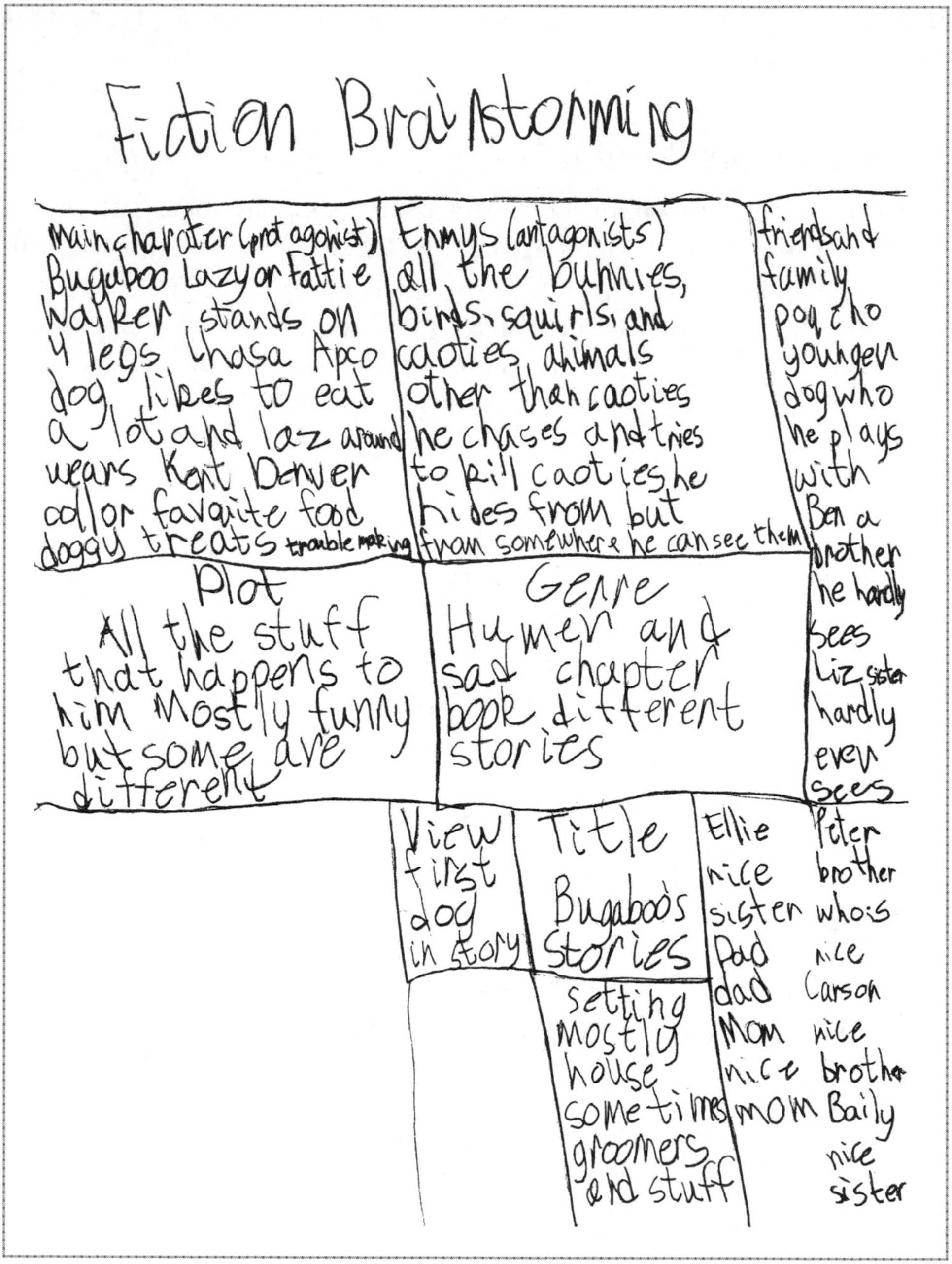

Fiction Brainstorming

main character (protagonist)
Bugaboo Lazy or Fattie Walker stands on 4 legs Lhasa Apco dog likes to eat a lot and laz around wears Kent Denver color favorite food doggy treats trouble making

Enmys (antagonists)
all the bunnies, birds, squirls, and caoties, animals other than caoties he chases and tries to kill caoties he hides from but from somewhere he can see them

friends and family
poq cho younger dog who he plays with Ben a brother he hardly sees Liz sister hardly even sees Peter brother who is nice Carson nice brother Baily nice sister

Plot
All the stuff that happens to him mostly funny but some are different

Genre
Humer and sad chapter book different stories

View
first dog in story

Title
Bugaboo's Stories

setting mostly house sometimes groomers and stuff

Ellie nice sister Dad dad Mom nice mom

Figure 3.4 Asonta's Storyboard Showing Her Planning for Her Piece

Let the kids lead the conferences! And always leave a conference teaching one thing that the writer needs.

Robert: Will you check in though?

Me: All you have to do is ask for a conference when I'm doing our status check. I'm really looking forward to this story.

Owning the Lesson

How do your students develop plot? How much time do they need to spend immersing themselves in fiction and narratives before writing a story themselves? What are the benefits of planning plot points ahead of time? All of this front-loading is time well spent: When students sit down to draft, they've already rehearsed and can get right to work.

What aspects of this lesson could you incorporate into your classroom? What types of books do your kids gravitate toward? Are certain books in your room never on the shelves, always in a student's hands? What kinds of books are students bringing into your classroom? How could you weave the plots of those books into your instruction?

Questions to Think About

- Do I let my students choose their plots? How do they decide what to write about?

- How much time do my students need to rehearse and plan their plots and talk about them with other students?

- Do my students change their plots as they draft and the story unfolds?

- What about students who begin a piece and then notice the plot is going nowhere? Can they change the direction? Abandon the piece and start over?

- What mentor texts are my students using to guide them when they choose a plot?

- Are my students trying to re-create movies, TV shows, or video games? How do I feel about that?

Leading Off

Introduction

After students have been introduced to the elements of fiction and have a plan in place, it's time to start writing. They need to know where to start—how to invite readers into the text and hold their attention. That's what good leads do. Readers today usually have short attention spans: You've got to "hook" them quickly. Gone are the days of *The Secret Garden*, in which the author spends the first hundred pages introducing the characters and the setting before anything happens.

But leads can be changed. Often writers go back to the beginning after they've been working on a piece for a while (or even after they've completed it) and change the lead. That's the joy of writing. Nothing is final until publication! Students need to know that's okay.

MENTOR TEXTS FOR STUDENTS

- Avi's *The True Confessions of Charlotte Doyle* (Orchard Books, 1990)
- Christopher Paul Curtis' *Bud, Not Buddy* (Random House, 1999)
- Roald Dahl's *Matilda* (Viking Kestrel, 1988)
- Sid Fleischman's *The Whipping Boy* (HarperCollins, 1986)
- Margaret Peterson Haddix's *Among the Hidden* (Simon & Schuster, 1998) and *Found* (Simon & Schuster, 2008)
- Liz Kessler's *The Tail of Emily Windsnap* (Candlewick, 2006)
- Madeline L'Engle's *A Wrinkle in Time* (Farrar, Straus and Giroux, 1962)
- Roland Smith's *Storm Runners* (Scholastic, 2011)

- Sarah Weeks' *So B. It* (HarperCollins, 2004)
- E. B. White's *Charlotte's Web* (HarperCollins, 1952)
- Jacqueline Woodson's *Feathers* (Penguin, 2007)

MATERIALS FOR STUDENTS
- Mentor text
- Story plan
- Writer's notebook
- Chart paper
- Books being read independently

TIME: 45 minutes

Here's How It Goes

"Think about the stories you really enjoy. How far do you usually read before you decide whether a book is going to be a good fit and interesting, or if it's going to be boring and you're going to drop it?" It's usually within a few pages, if that. A few kids say they'll read a chapter before deciding.

"Today we're going to pull out our independent reading books and read like writers. These are books you've decided to continue reading, so the writer 'hooked' you—pulled you into the story. Read the first sentence and then the first paragraph to yourself and think about how the author captures your interest. That's reading like a writer. What does the author do?"

After students do this independently, I have them share the leads and their thinking with their group (usually four students). Then we come back together as a class and share and write on an anchor chart what we notice about great leads.

"I have a couple other examples of leads that I think are great. I'm going to read them to you. Notice what the author is doing, and decide whether they catch your attention." I read the first two paragraphs of *So B. It*, by Sarah Weeks:

If truth was a crayon and it was up to me to put a wrapper around it and name its color, I know just what I would call it—**dinosaur skin**. I used to think, without really thinking about it, that I knew what color that was. But that was a long time ago, before I knew what I know now about both dinosaur skin and the truth.

> The fact is, you can't tell squat about the color of an animal just from look-
> ing at its bones, so nobody knows for sure what color dinosaurs really were.
> For years I looked at pictures of them, trusting that whoever was in charge
> of coloring them in was doing it based on scientific fact, but the truth is
> they were only guessing. I realized that one afternoon, sitting in the front
> seat of Sheriff Roy Franklin's squad car, the fall before I turned thirteen.

"This lead opens up a whole lot of questions for us about both truth and the color of dinosaurs. Plus it leaves us wondering what happened when the character was thirteen and sitting in the squad car."

Then I read the first three sentences of *Found*, by Margaret Peterson Haddix:

> It wasn't there. Then it was.
>
> Later, that was how Angela DuPre would describe the airplane—over and
> over, to one investigator after another—until she was told never to speak
> of it again.

"How about that for a lead? Two short sentences and the visual of an airplane suddenly appearing, then someone being told never to speak of it again—intrigue at its best!"

Next I read the "Important Warning" that begins *The True Confessions of Charlotte Doyle*, by Avi:

> Not every thirteen-year-old girl is accused of murder, brought to trial,
> and found guilty. But I was just such a girl, and my story is worth relating
> even if it did happen years ago. Be warned, however, this is no **Story of a
> Bad Boy**, no **What Katy Did**. If strong ideas and action offend you, read
> no more. Find another companion to share your idle hours. For my part I
> intend to tell the truth as I lived it.

"In this lead Avi introduces us to the main character, shocks us, provides foreshadowing, and teases us to continue reading only if we can handle it!"

"Roland Smith begins *Storm Runners* like this":

> **When my father got struck by lightning, so did I,** Chase thought. **When
> Mom and Monica died, so did I . . . a little. . . .**

"Smith lets us into the thoughts of his main character—with a shock, leaving us asking many questions.

"And here's the beginning of *The Tail of Emily Windsnap*, by Liz Kessler:

Can you keep a secret?

Everybody has secrets, of course, but mine's different, and it's kind of weird. Sometimes I even have nightmares that people will find out about it and lock me up in a zoo or a scientist's laboratory.

"Kessler begins with a question—a question that intrigues all of us. Then she makes us wonder what her secret is. Are you hooked?"

Of course I have to end with a classic. There are so many wonderful leads appropriate for this lesson, but E. B. White was a master:

"Where's Papa going with that ax?" said Fern to her mother as they were setting the table for breakfast.

A farmer doesn't carry an ax unless he's going to use it!

"Now it's your turn. Take a look at all the work you've done so far planning your piece and think about how you might want to start. What kind of lead would work for your piece? Let's try a few. Your job now is to write at least three different leads."

Students do this independently and then confer with a partner. Often students like aspects of each of the three and end up combining them into a fourth. Here is Emma's beginning of her story about Bubba the elephant:

High up on the green-covered plains of Madagascar, the ground rumbled as if an earthquake was slowly rolling in. The animals scattered in all directions: some ostriches running into each other with wild monkeys steering them on their backs . . . but it was only Bubba trying to make some friends.

As you read Anna's lead, imagine what type of fiction she reads:

"Student 343, wake up!" A voice spiraled up the staircase. "Student 343, if you don't wake up you'll miss your studies!" Someone shouted again, their tone rising. A girl sat up and roused herself out of her old fashioned bed. She bent over, her dirty hands covering her tear-washed face. Oh, she thought, drenched in a pool of despair, I've been at this home for ten years now. And yet, I still haven't been adopted. It will never happen! I might as well run away. I've been thinking about it for years. I loathe this place, I loathe being called Student 343, and I loathe my studies! Then the tears came, cascading down Student 343's cheeks and soaking her white on white pajama's. With a click, a skinny woman blundered into the room and spun around to face the weeping girl.

"Student 343," the woman's red lips spat the words like they had a foul taste. Her tone was dripping poison. "Where have you been? You'll get us both in trouble if you don't come along." The woman spoke with a faint accent that couldn't be placed.

At the end of these two paragraphs, most readers are full of questions and want to read on.

Geoffrey was fascinated with the ghost lore in Colorado history and read as many books on haunting as we could find. His favorite was about the ghosts at the Stanley Hotel, in Estes Park (where Stephen King wrote *The Shining*). Geoffrey eases his readers into his ghost story slowly:

Way back in 1852, there was a famous hotel named Hotel des Moines—a French hotel in Quebec, Canada. It was so famous because there had been a rumor that ghosts had been sighted. Hotel des Moines was very big, so ghosts could sneak around in pretty much any room. But the room that people saw ghosts in most was room 1141—a room on the top floor. 1141 was a guest suite. I am telling you this story because I was a resident at Hotel des Moines—on the top floor in room 1141. Yes, reader, you might be asking if I spotted any ghosts, but you will have to hold your nerves and wait until the end of this book. If you want to know, read on.

Pressing Your Advantage

Often I have students continue to work on their leads the next day in writing workshop. They take one of the three leads they wrote the day before and rewrite it three times, adding details, refining word choice, tweaking, polishing. They "zoom in" on the description or the action.

In the lesson above, students work in groups, sharing leads in the books they are reading independently. As another follow-up option, I ask students to bring in one more example of a terrific lead by the end of the week and be prepared to read it and explain why it's effective. Or I create a "lead board" where students post awesome leads. (This becomes a wall of book recommendations; students hooked by a lead read the book.)

When Kids Don't Get It

Even with the support of mentor texts and lots of examples, some students either don't know how to start or don't want to. This is a perfect time to pull together a needs group and present the "lifting lines" lesson (lesson 8), this time lifting leads. I write a lead sentence from a mentor text on the board, and students use the structure as a model to craft a sentence to begin the narrative on which they're working.

One-to-One

Robert has written three leads:

> Once there was a boy named Mac who was a bully.
> A long time ago Mac lived in a village.
> Mac was a boy who didn't have any friends.

I check in.

Me: How's it going?

Robert: Fine. I wrote three leads.

Me: And what do you think? Do you notice anything?

Robert: I made sure my character was in the lead. You said character was important.

Me: Yes, I did. I can tell you paid attention. Now I'm going to ask you another question. If you read these sentences in a book, would you want to keep reading? Do they grab your attention?

Robert: No. But they're only one sentence.

Me: Great observation! And you're right. A lead can be much longer. So why don't we work on that? How about if we turn your lead into a lead paragraph?

Robert: How do I do that?

Me: We keep expanding on what you've written. When I read your leads, I think maybe you wanted to start by setting up your character. Is that right? Or did you want to start with some action?

Robert: I want to start with Mac.

Me: Great. How about if you keep telling me what Mac would be doing at the beginning of the story. Why he doesn't have friends and why he's a bully. As you talk, I'll jot down what you say. Then we can go back and pull out pieces to put in your lead.

Robert: That works.

Robert begins to share. It requires a lot of nudging and questioning on my part, but Robert begins to set up his character and the problems that Mac faces. I do the writing. Writing is tough for Robert, and I want to capture his thinking, so he can go back and choose what to include. He will be able to take the sentences I have scribed and embed them into his draft, although I also expect him to add his own details and thinking.

Owning the Lesson

Starting is always hard. It helps to give students a strong foundation with lots of examples. This lesson is based on noticing what effective authors do: Students use mentor texts to craft their own leads. How is this different from story starters or formulaic leads? What works for you and for your students?

Do you struggle with beginnings in your own writing? How could you share that with your students? Could you use students' writing from previous years to model writing effective leads? (Often my students say they learn as much, if not more, from looking at other students' writing.) Is studying leads a one-time lesson or could you use it several times during the school year to notice leads in a variety of texts?

Questions to Think About

- How often do my students think about the leads in the books they are reading, noticing what the author does to hook them?
- Do my students have opportunities to explicitly identify what authors do to create strong leads?
- How often do I emphasize leads and beginnings in all genres?

- How could I use this lesson in other units or with other genres?
- How much choice do my students have over their leads?
- Do my students have opportunities to revise leads or change leads when they are drafting?
- How are leads different from topic sentences?

Writing Under the Influence
Drafting, Revising, and Editing

Introduction

Most of the time now is spent writing, but I present a few minilessons (small group or whole class) and have a lot of conferences. There are also a lot of peer conferences. As a writing teacher, I realize students will be in different places in the writing process along the way. That's why the status of the class is paramount. I can quickly ascertain where each student is and teach the writer.

MENTOR TEXTS FOR STUDENTS

It's up to you! Your students are drafting, revising, and editing. What books are they modeling their writing on?

MATERIALS FOR STUDENTS

- Mentor text
- Writer's notebook
- Writing folder or portfolio
- Dictionaries, thesauruses, other resources, computers

TIME: Final two weeks of the unit

Here's How It Goes

"Before I turn you loose to write today, I want to show you one more graphic organizer. Remember 'Utah Flipped'? Here's another one that will remind you of the three parts of writing stories."

I pull out the following anchor chart:

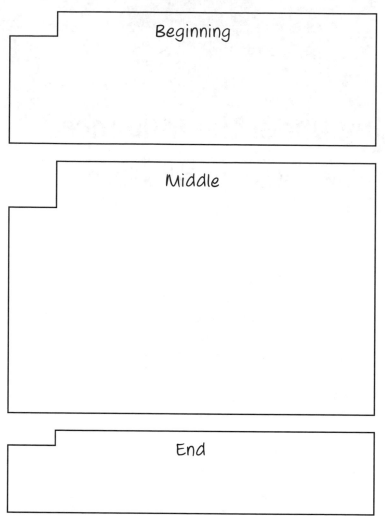

"What do you notice?"

Maddie answers, "It has three boxes. Does that mean we only write three paragraphs?"

"Great question. No, you get to determine how many paragraphs, but you must have a minimum of three. A beginning, a middle, and an end. What do you notice about the boxes?"

"The top and bottom ones are thinner," Jack observes.

"Why?"

"Are we supposed to write less there?" Reed suggests.

"You got it. The first box is the beginning or lead, where you grab your reader's attention right away. Then you move into the middle, which is the thick box, and finally finish with the end. You already worked on leads, so you could put the lead you chose in the beginning box and any other details you want to include to introduce your reader to your narrative.

"I'm going to leave this chart up on the wall, and if you want to draw one like it in your writer's notebook and fill it out, you can. If you think you're ready to write, go to it. Let's write for the period, but stop when there are fifteen minutes left to confer with a partner about what you've written."

Erin doesn't want to use my graphic organizer, preferring to sketch out her piece on a storyboard (see Figure 3.5). She revises her notes and leaves notes to herself about final illustrations. Each student approaches writing differently and needs the power to choose.

Figure 3.5 Erin's Storyboard

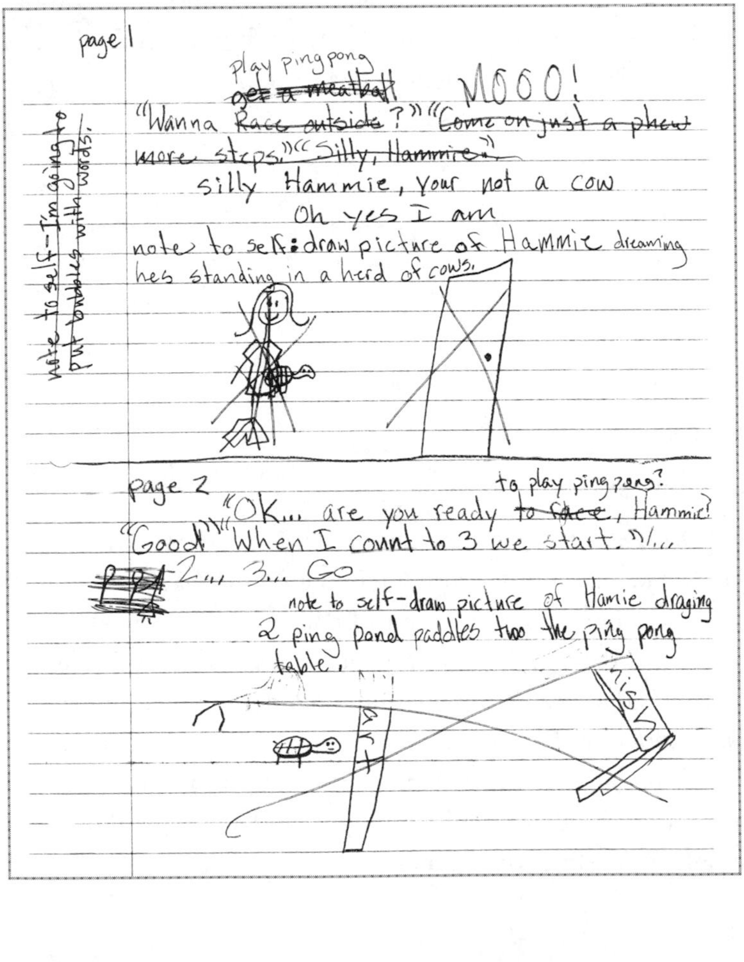

Pressing Your Advantage

I no longer let students confer with classmates throughout the workshop. I used to, but there was always some talking in the room—quiet talking, but talking nonetheless. Many students need silence to think and write, and I want to allow for all types of learning styles in my classroom. We talk, we move, and then we work silently, which requires stamina.

Now I build in time either at the beginning or end of workshop for peer conferences. Conferring at the beginning helps set up the work for the day. Conferring at the end wraps it up, encourages reflection, and identifies next steps for the following day. Stepping back and thinking about the process is especially valuable when writing fiction.

When Kids Don't Get It

This far into the unit, I know which students still need support with organization. In small groups or individual conferences, I re-create the beginning, middle, end graphic organizer, adding a 1, 2, and 3 to the middle box to help them plan three events that will occur in the middle of their story.

One-to-One

Another visit with Robert.

> **Me:** How's it going?
>
> **Robert:** I've been writing. I've been using the plan.
>
> **Me:** Do you want help with anything?
>
> **Robert:** Not right now, I want to write.

What Robert had written so far was minimal: *Mac was a 16 year old boy. He lived a long time ago in a town. One day in school he got in trouble and he ran away. He ran to the forest.* There are many things I could work on with Robert. He has taken some of the work we did earlier on leads, and I could push him to add more, embed what I had scripted. But he's had a conference every day and he wants to work *independently*. He's in the writing zone. I want to honor his independence—this is a huge step. There will be plenty of opportunities later on to teach. By listening to him and allowing him to work, I'm facilitating that independence. Sometimes the best thing we can do is to get out of the way!

Owning the Lesson

How much time do your students need to finish up this unit of study? Because they've done so much planning and rehearsing, they should now be able to write. I've allotted two weeks for students to complete the writing process and turn in a final draft; what makes sense for you and your students?

Are there things you want to continue to work on as students draft? Or is it more beneficial to allow students to write and confer? Where will you be? Conferring with students or working with small groups or a combination of both?

Questions to Think About

- Are there other aspects of narrative or fiction writing that I want to teach in this unit?

- Do my students know how to work through the writing process: drafting, revising, and editing their work?

- Do my students have times in which they can confer with one another?

- How do I know what my students are working on each day? How do they let me know if they need help?

- What happens when my students start a draft and find it's not a workable idea? What options do they have? Are they allowed to start over?

- Do my students periodically reflect on how they're doing in the process?

- What about my students who finish early? What do they work on when the class is writing silently?

Wrapping It Up

Endings in Narratives

Introduction

Ending a piece of writing can be one of the hardest things to do. When I was in school, I found ending anything I wrote brutally difficult. I just wanted to be done. So many student pieces end "And she woke up and it was all a dream" or simply "The End." But a satisfying ending encourages readers to think about what they've just read. As the majority of my students begin to wrap up their first draft, it's time to pull out the mentor texts and dive into reading great endings.

MENTOR TEXTS FOR STUDENTS

- The most powerful way to demonstrate explicitly how endings tie back to beginnings is to examine the beginning and the ending of the same book. Use the same mentor texts you used in lesson 15 and have students notice the connections between the lead and the ending.

- Picture books also contain great examples. Any books by Chris Van Allsburg are excellent choices (his books often end with a twist that the reader has to figure out). Some of my favorites are *The Stranger* (Houghton Mifflin, 1986), *The Garden of Abdul Gasazi* (Houghton Mifflin, 1979), *Jumanji* (Houghton Mifflin, 1981), and *The Wreck of the Zephyr* (Houghton Mifflin, 1983).

MATERIALS FOR STUDENTS

- Mentor text
- Story drafts

TIME: 45 minutes

Here's How It Goes

"Today we're going to take a look at how narratives end. I know many of you are getting ready to wrap up your drafts, so it's time to notice how other authors write great endings. Have you ever read a book where the ending disappointed you?"

Heads nod.

"I have, too. Do you remember what it was about the ending that you didn't like?"

"It just ended. Everything was going great and then the author just quit."

"My questions didn't get answered."

"The action totally dropped off."

"I didn't understand it."

"I agree with all of those. We know what we don't like, now we need to look at what we do like. Today I'm going to share endings from some of the same books we looked at for leads, to see what the authors do. I'm also assigning you homework for tomorrow. I want you to bring in a book whose ending you loved. It can be any book. I want you to be prepared to share the conclusion or ending and explain what the author did. Remember how we are reading like writers. That's your job for tomorrow.

"Some books I finish, when I put them down I can't seem to get the story out of my head. It's like I've lost a good friend. The story was that memorable. Endings really reinforce how we remember a book. Sometimes endings are beginnings. Have you ever finished a book and continued the story in your imagination?"

Again, many students nod in agreement.

I share endings from books we've delved into earlier and we begin to chart different types of endings on a class anchor chart. Students come up with ideas such as:

- It ends with characters' feelings.
- The ending circles back to the beginning.
- There's an epilogue or an after-part that goes into the future and explains what happens to all of the characters. [The final Harry Potter book is an excellent example of this!]
- There is a moral or lesson. A decision is made.
- The final action happens.
- It leaves you hanging or you have to make an inference.
- It launches a new story. [This often happens in series.]

- It surprises the reader. [This is a mainstay of mysteries.]
- It leaves you in a good mood or with a good feeling.

The lesson ends with the expectation that the following day students will be bringing in examples of their own.

Pressing Your Advantage

The next day we follow through on the homework assignment. Students, in small groups, share the ending of the book they brought in and explain what the author did to make it satisfying and memorable. We add any new types of endings to the anchor chart. The chart is a helpful reference for students who are struggling with their ending. I also use this chart as a resource during conferences, asking students what type of ending they envision for their piece and why.

When Kids Don't Get It

I still have students who write "The End" to let the reader know they're done. Working with them individually tends to be more beneficial than pulling together a needs group. I draw their attention to our anchor chart and have them choose one of the types of endings for their piece. Then we find mentor texts that match that type and study the author's craft together. Sometimes we'll lift an ending to use as a model.

The easier endings to write are:

- How the character feels at the end.
- A final decision or lesson that the character learned.
- The culminating action of the plot.
- Circling back to the beginning of the story.

One-to-One

Robert's first draft has a beginning and a middle with some action; Mac finds the dragon, the two of them return to the village, and the dragon breathes fire and drives the "bad guys" out of town. He ends with, *After the bad guys ran away Mac went back to the village*.

Me: So you finished up all the action. Mac and the dragon saved the town. How do you like your ending?

Robert: It's happy, Mac comes back.

Me: Do you think your readers might have any questions? Do you think you've wrapped your story up so that they understand?

Robert: I don't know. Maybe.

Me: Can we try something different? Would you mind conferring with Sydney and Ben on your piece, since they are done with their drafts? Ask them to focus on your ending and see whether they have any questions for you, things they're not sure of. After you've done that, think about their questions. I'll come back later and we'll see if there's anything you want to do with your piece.

I could have asked Robert questions about his ending, but he would have been getting feedback from the same person he'd been getting it from all along. I wanted him to hear it from his peers. I knew Ben and Sydney had the time to confer with Robert and would give him helpful responses. I also knew Robert respected Ben's and Sydney's thinking. And I wanted him to work with a boy and a girl to get different perspectives. Ben and Sydney were honest with Robert. They wanted to know where the dragon was and what happened with Mac and the dragon at the end. They wanted to know whether Mac was still a bully.

When they finished, I stopped by Robert's desk again and asked how it went. He shared what they had talked about and I asked which questions he thought were important—which ones he might work on to make the ending better. He talked about the dragon and how it went back to the woods but he and Mac were friends forever. I could have pushed Robert to address the bully question too, but I wanted to keep it simple.

Me: So, it's kind of like you're wrapping this up with a final action and how the characters feel about each other, right?

Robert: Yes.

Me: Do you want to try it on your own? And then maybe meet back with Sydney and Ben to get their feedback? And of course you know I'll keep checking in!

Owning the Lesson

As always, I urge you to think about your own writing. How do you approach endings? And think about your reading. Do you notice how authors wrap up their books, especially the ones that are memorable? Is this lesson something you present in your reading workshop as well as your writing workshop? Could you teach literary terms such as *climax* and *resolution* while you're teaching endings? How does this lesson apply to other genres and other subjects?

Questions to Think About

- Can I use this lesson with other genres and other areas of the curriculum? How do authors conclude or end informative and persuasive writing?
- Do my students know how authors craft endings? Can they state labels or definitions for the different ways narratives end?
- Do I let my students choose how they will end their story? Does the ending fit with the story?
- Do my students have opportunities to draft different endings for their piece and choose the one they think is best?

Finalizing, Reflecting, Going Public, and Celebrating!

Introduction

Students have made the deadline and now it's time to share. An audience is important, as is knowing the stories are going somewhere other than my desk for a grade. Authors write to have their words read.

The first part of this lesson focuses on reflection, an essential way in which we solidify learning, acknowledge the risks we took, and recognize how we've changed as writers. Then we go public. I invite the principal to walk through the room and see what the students have written.

MENTOR TEXTS

- The kids work, of course!
- It's even better when the students display their mentor text next to the final product. What a great connection!

MATERIALS FOR STUDENTS

- Final draft of fiction piece
- Earlier drafts, notebook entries, planning sheets
- Reflection sheet

TIME: 30 minutes for reflection; 30 minutes to "walk the room"

Here's How It Goes

It's the day the stories are due, and the kids come in with their finished pieces. They know everyone is going to read everyone else's piece, and no one wants to be left out. Before we share our writing, though, I ask students for a final reflection:

- How did you get the idea for your piece?

- What mentor text informed your writing? How did you use this text?

- How did you create your character? How did your character turn out?

- Explain how you *revised* your piece. Give two specific examples of how you made revision decisions and how they changed your writing.

- How did you *edit* your piece so that it was audience-ready?

- What did you learn about writing fiction? What did you learn about yourself as a writer?

- Score yourself using the six-traits rubric.

Students also give me "editorial" directions, because I'll be preparing their pieces for display. Do they want their story bound? Laminated? Special requests? This is the time to tell me.

Finally we walk from table to table, reading, reading, reading. Nothing is heard except the sound of pages turning. No talking, no commenting. Just soaking in our stories. It isn't over until everyone has finished reading. This is too important, and the kids value it too much. Finally, we give ourselves a round of applause and offer comments to our classmates. It's magical!

Ben wrote a piece about being a famous child hockey star. He and I had many conferences about making the piece understandable for someone who didn't know the ins and outs of hockey the way he did and making it believable. Here are his reflections:

> I did sports and humor fiction. My mentor text was that I like hockey, and it was my mind, because you have to use your imagination while writing fiction. I had to make sure that someone that didn't play hockey would understand the story. Also I had to make some stuff make sense. Like [the main character] having a guardian and a tutor. I found that fiction is

▶ THE NITTY-GRITTY

Celebrations with students can extend to celebrations with parents. If the timing is right, students can display their writing in the classroom during parent-teacher conferences. Or you can hold an evening open house after students have completed several units of study, and invite parents to come in and read student writing. Or you can organize an evening of poetry slams. Whatever values and celebrates the writing and increases the audience.

very hard to write. It was hard to make someone understand it because a lot of people don't know anything about hockey.

Ben took a lot of risks with his piece, and he revised and revised and then revised some more. Conferences nudged him to make his piece better. He writes that fiction is hard, but he also worked incredibly hard at making his piece as good as possible.

Here are some of Ellie's reflections:

I wrote a humor and fantasy book. I didn't really have a mentor text—I just thought of the funny books I like and some of the dog picture books Mrs. B. has read, but I had a mentor dog. My mentor dog was my own dog because the story was from his point of view. It was a humor book because it was about the problems my dog got into and it was a fantasy because it was from a dog's point of view. It helped me as a writer because last year we had to write a fiction story and it was hard for me. I couldn't think at all in it and in this one I was able to do it because I had a plan and envisioned it.

I learned that I could do fiction. The only thing that I had trouble with was writing long chapters. It was easy to write fiction because I was able to think of things to write and I never wanted to start over.

And Trinity's:

I wrote a genre of realistic fiction because my mentor text was **The Spirit of Endurance**. I think this helped me understand fiction and how to make things more exciting. I usually write poetry, so this was a big change for me. I had my sister, brother and parents listen and read it to help me revise and edit. It really helped when Mrs. B. conferred with me, but I did most of this on my own. I think I learned that fiction is hard, but if you find a good genre it can be less difficult. There is no way that I could have written something funny.

Sydney's reflections are shown in Figure 3.6. She evaluates herself as a writer, then scores herself using the six-traits rubric (by this time students understand each trait and the scoring system). I also score Sydney. The goal is for our scores to be identical.

A large discrepancy is a perfect segue to a conference in which we discuss how the student views the writing and why she or he scored it a certain way and how I view the writing and why I assigned the scores I did. I want the students to internalize the rubrics—to know when they are writing quality work, to no longer have to ask, "Is this good enough?" If they understand the rubric, they can answer that question on their own.

Figure 3.6 Sydney's reflection and self-evaluation. Notice how Sydney realizes that creating characters was easier for her than developing plot.

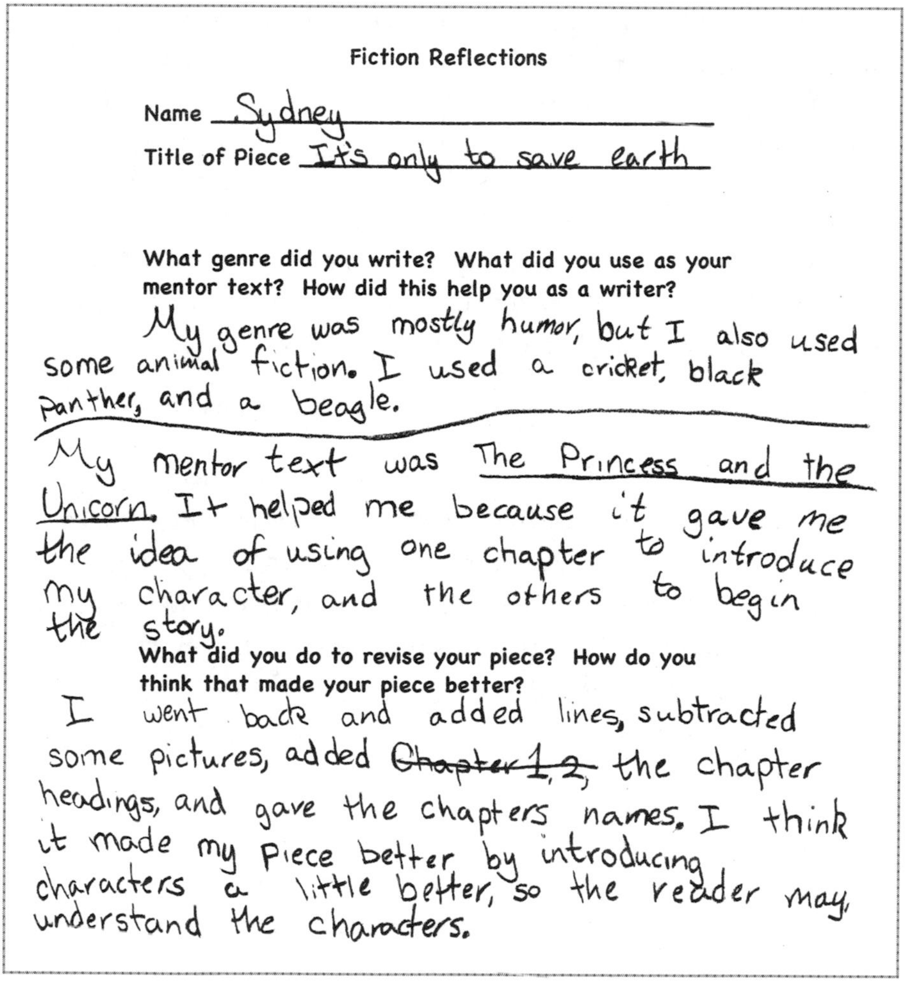

Fiction Reflections

Name Sydney

Title of Piece It's only to save earth

What genre did you write? What did you use as your mentor text? How did this help you as a writer?

My genre was mostly humor, but I also used some animal fiction. I used a cricket, black panther, and a beagle.

My mentor text was The Princess and the Unicorn. It helped me because it gave me the idea of using one chapter to introduce my character, and the others to begin the story.

What did you do to revise your piece? How do you think that made your piece better?

I went back and added lines, subtracted some pictures, added ~~Chapter 1, 2~~ the chapter headings, and gave the chapters names. I think it made my piece better by introducing characters a little better, so the reader may understand the characters.

Figure 3.6 Continued

> **What did you learn about yourself as a writer as you worked on this fiction unit? What was easy for you and what was hard?**
>
> I learned that I can easily write fiction, and I'm able to have fun with it. Coming up with characters was easy, but making the story was hard.
>
> **What did you do to edit your final piece?**
>
> I used spell check on the computer, and my skill to edit it. I went back through and decided to what to edit and what to keep.
>
> **Score yourself (1 – 5):**
>
> Organization _____ 4
>
> Ideas and Content _____ 4
>
> Sentence Fluency _____ 4
>
> Voice _____ 5
>
> Word Choice _____ 4
>
> Grammar and Conventions _____ 4

Pressing Your Advantage

The unit is finished. What's next? Of course I need to respond to the student's reflections and evaluate their papers. I use a rubric, but I also write a reflection of my own for each student—what I noticed about their process, the risks they took, what shines in their writing, what they learned. Lucie and Rachael, who were afraid of taking risks, took them and grew as writers; they were successful, and I'm going to write that to them. These written reflections from me mean more than the numbers on a rubric. They honor the writer.

I also laminate, bind, and otherwise prepare their pieces for display. If they're too heavy to hang in the hall, we find other ways to display them. Often our stories remain in the classroom in bins or on shelves for students to continue to enjoy. And they take them home at the end of the year!

When Kids Don't Get It

When a student turns in a piece that is not audience-ready I need to step in and teach. I have the student come in at lunch, and we edit the piece together. If the student is capable of it, I ask them to refinalize the piece and turn it back in. For students who struggle with writing, I often type the final piece after we edit together. I want everyone to be successful!

When Kids Forget Their Piece or Haven't Quite Finished

It happens. But after kids have experienced one walk-the-room celebration, they are rarely late again. If they are, they make themselves accountable.

Madison had finished her story but left it at home and her mother wasn't able to deliver it until later in the morning. She left a handwritten sign on her desk: "Please stop by after recess, my piece will be here and I'd love you to read it!"

Conner wasn't finished finalizing his piece. He left a note on his rough draft: "Please feel free to read my rough draft. My final will be done at lunch!"

These students don't need me nagging them. They want their classmates to know what happened. They've worked hard, and they want to be part of the celebration. Because it is a celebration. Kids honor one another and their accomplishments. They honor *everyone*, no matter his or her ability, because we're all writers and we're all in it together!

Owning the Lesson

Our words and our actions have power. What we say and do conveys so much to our students. So when we linger and celebrate and honor risks (and failures), students will continue to take those risks and grow as writers.

In this lesson students have time to read each other's work; they hold one another accountable. Who owns your classroom? Are your students writing to please you or a greater audience?

How can you take pieces of this lesson and apply them in your classroom? Celebrations? Student reflections? Rubrics? Response to writing? How do you continue to raise the bar so that your students push themselves to excel?

Questions to Think About

- How are my student's final pieces made public?

- Who is the public? Me or a greater audience?

- How do I hold my students accountable?

- How is writing—especially taking risks—celebrated?

- Do I give my students time to reflect, to truly think about what they attempted and what they did well, to articulate how they used mentor texts to inform their own writing?

- How do I give feedback to my students? Through rubrics? Through written comments? When students read my comments, are they motivated to write more?

Wrap-Up

When we let students choose what they want to write, what do they usually pick? Fiction. And then they start and stop, because it's hard. Because they love to read fiction, they turn to it in their writing, expecting it to be as easy as their reading. It isn't. But when we teach it explicitly—and tie that instruction to mentor texts—we can give our students experience writing narratives.

Some authors write fiction; some write columns, humor, nonfiction, whatever. Let's expose our students to all these genres. They can experience success and frustration. We're cheating them if we don't let them see the wide variety of writing, and fiction is part of that. Although the majority of our students won't grow up to be John Grisham or Jodi Picoult, they need to see what fiction writers do. And we need to support them as they attempt different genres and take risks. If our students only play it safe, they won't grow.

This cluster of lessons is a unit of study. You could present specific lessons in isolation, but they work together to enhance the study of fiction or narrative writing. When I finish this unit of study, many students say how difficult it turned out to be, yet they always love doing it, perhaps because it gives them new insight into what their favorite fiction authors are doing to hold their interest. Fiction ain't easy, but when we read great fiction it feels seamless. What an art!

What About Assessment?

Lesson 18 includes student reflection and self-scoring. Student input is an important part of the assessment/grading process. I assess my students using the six-traits writing rubric, but I also assess them on their reflections and what they attempted. My assessment is a mix of informal (conferences, use of class time, reflections) and formal—the six-traits rubric on their final piece. How could this unit of study be used to assess the components of the CCSS writing, reading, and language standards?

What Else?

In Lesson Cluster One, students learned how to write *narrative paragraphs*. This unit of study builds on those lessons. Students are already familiar with what a narrative is. They are used to telling and writing stories. They read stories all the time. This unit of study allows them to notice their own reading and incorporate what they notice into a piece of writing. It also gives them a greater appreciation for fiction writers.

What else could you do in this unit? Think technology.

If a goal for you is to assess the CCSS speaking standards, students could do an audio or video podcast. If you don't have access to technology but want to emphasize speaking, students could read their pieces to children in lower grades.

If you want your students to publish their work in a different format, a digital storybook, for example, check out StoryJumper (www.storyjumper.com). If you want your students to publish a book that they can have bound and take home, check out Lintor Make-a-Book products (www.lintorpublishing.com/default.php).

Things to Think About

- Fiction and narratives are part of my reading workshop. How does teaching a fiction unit of study fit into my writing workshop?

- How are these lessons different from the fiction lessons I've taught before?

- Which of these lessons would benefit my students and improve their writing? What do my students do well, and what do they need support to be able to do?

- How do I turn choice in fiction or narrative writing over to my students and encourage them to take risks?

- How do I explicitly teach the elements of fiction in reading workshop? In writing workshop?

- How can I use the concept of mentor texts to enhance writing instruction, especially because students have a great deal of exposure to fiction?

Writing Nonfiction

Getting Beyond the Five-Paragraph Theme

19. Gathering Texts
20. Launching an Inquiry Study
21. Making Expectations Explicit
22. Becoming Experts
23. Asking Questions to Guide Research
24. Determining Importance of Ideas in Texts
25. Developing Voice While Taking Notes
26. Envisioning Texts
27. Using Paragraphs Effectively
28. Writing Leads
29. Organizing Ideas
30. Drafting, Editing, and Revising
31. Presenting and Sharing Students' Texts and Knowledge

Faced with writing nonfiction, students often crank out dull, lifeless pieces. But the excerpts below demonstrate what happens when students are immersed in language, know what makes terrific writing, understand content, and can connect it all while writing about a topic they've chosen. (I can't stress *choice* enough here.)

Cacti

Let's imagine that you are a saguaro cactus seed. Where's your mother and father? You don't have any, but you are lucky because you have a nurse. A nurse tree. The nurse tree helps keep you from being eaten and run over when you are a few years old.

In the future, when you are at 150 years old, you will stand in the sun like a green poky person, but right now you are just a seed and you don't know that in a few years you will grow **a little**. You feast on the jungle forty or fifty feet below you. If you turn the desert upside down, then it would look like a jungle underneath.

—MacKenzie (fifth grader)

Roller Coasters

Click . . . Click . . . Click . . . You're near the top of the hill. All of a sudden, you shoot backwards. You hear a recording repeating, "Malfunction! Malfunction!" You level out and jerk to a stop. Your best friend Jacob is shocked, just like you.

You luckily stop at the station, where the roller coaster starts and ends. Jacob says, "Okay, that was the freakiest thing I've ever done." You both hop out of the train.

"I want to talk to somebody who knows a lot about roller coasters and see what he has to say about roller-coaster accidents," you say.

—Taylor (fourth grader)

Being in Mexico

Hola, I'm going to Mexico it's going to be fun! But I need to learn some facts about Mexico. I read really good books, but now I need to discover other things about Mexico like the flag, the president, and holidays. So I better write this down.

Have you ever wondered how the Mexican flag looked like? Well, I will tell you how it looks, what it used to represent, and what it means now.

—Oscar (ESL third grader)

Notice how different the leads are? They reflect the breadth of the students' mentor texts. These essays are also the result of research. Every year my students undertake at least one research project, or *inquiry study*. My classroom was one of those Stephanie Harvey wrote about in *Nonfiction Matters* (1998).

Generally I can conduct two research studies during the year. The first study takes a much longer time, because I'm scaffolding and setting the groundwork. The second go-round moves at a faster clip, because kids know the expectations and, more importantly, know how to access and comprehend nonfiction. For the past few years, I've had students write a feature article (like those they've been reading in *Time for Kids*) as the culminating product of their research.

Aligning Your Instruction with the Common Core State Standards

According to the reading standards, 50 percent of student texts should be non-fiction. Therefore, we should be teaching a lot of nonfiction and surrounding our students with a wide variety of nonfiction text. I use mentor texts in all these lessons, but I do not explicitly match individual lessons with specific Common Core State Standards (CCSS) reading standards.

Informative/explanatory writing and the research process are the focus of this section. In addition, speaking, listening, and language skills are all integral to writing and presenting a research article.

COLLEGE AND CAREER READINESS ANCHOR STANDARDS FOR WRITING

TEXT TYPES AND PURPOSES

1. Write informative/explanatory texts to examine and convey complex ideas and information clearly and accurately through the effective selection, organization, and analysis of content.

Students write well-developed pieces that include details and accurate facts. They analyze information and in some cases offer arguments or write thesis statements.

PRODUCTION AND DISTRIBUTION OF WRITING

2. Produce clear and coherent writing in which the development, organization, and style are appropriate to task, purpose, and audience.

3. Develop and strengthen writing as needed by planning, revising, editing, rewriting, or trying a new approach.

Students work through the entire writing process to finalize a piece.

RESEARCH TO BUILD AND PRESENT KNOWLEDGE

4. Conduct short as well as more sustained research projects based on focused questions, demonstrating understanding of the subject under investigation.

5. Gather relevant information from multiple print and digital sources, assess the credibility and accuracy of each source, and integrate the information while avoiding plagiarism.

6. Draw evidence from literary or informational texts to support analysis, reflection, and research.

The lessons in this section show how to set up a research study and formulate questions, how to take notes, and then how to put it all together in final form. Although most of the lessons are based on printed mentor texts, students also use digital sources.

RANGE OF WRITING

7. Write routinely over extended time frames (time for research, reflection, and revision) and shorter time frames (a single sitting or a day or two) for a range of tasks, purposes, and audiences.

Students have weeks of workshop time to draft and finalize their pieces, which is definitely writing over extended time frames!

COLLEGE AND CAREER READINESS ANCHOR STANDARDS FOR READING

RANGE OF READING AND LEVEL OF TEXT COMPLEXITY

8. Read and comprehend complex literary and informational texts independently and proficiently.

The first lesson in this section is on gathering texts to read independently and proficiently. As students choose their own texts for their research topics, they continue to address this standard.

Lesson 19

Gathering Texts

Introduction

If my students are to write quality nonfiction pieces, I need to expose them to a variety of well-written nonfiction. At least two weeks before we begin drafting our nonfiction pieces—or even earlier—I begin reading nonfiction to them in connection with minilessons highlighting variety, structure, and beautiful language. Every year, I bring in different examples to share with my class.

MENTOR TEXTS FOR TEACHERS

- Ralph Fletcher and Joann Portalupi's *Nonfiction Craft Lessons* (2001)
- Stephanie Harvey's *Nonfiction Matters* (1998)
- Katie Wood Ray's *Study Driven: A Framework for Planning Units of Study in the Writing Workshop* (2006)

THE LANGUAGE OF LEARNING

I was so fortunate to work with Steph Harvey through the Public Education and Business Coalition. She was a phenomenal mentor, and I'm proud that many of the examples in *Nonfiction Matters* came from my classes. I refer to the book often in these lessons, and I encourage you to pick up *Nonfiction Matters* for an in-depth look at nonfiction writing.

MENTOR TEXTS FOR STUDENTS

- Eve Bunting's *I Am the Mummy Heb Nefert* (Harcourt, 1997)
- Malachy Doyle's *Cow* (Margaret K. McElderry, 2002)

- Meredith Hooper's *Antarctic Journal* (National Geographic Society, 2000)
- Bert Kitchen's *Animal Lives: The Barn Owl* (Kingfisher, 1999) and *Somewhere Today* (Candlewick, 1992)
- Ted Lewin's *Lost City: The Discovery of Machu Picchu* (Penguin Putnam, 2003)
- Patricia Lauber's *Hurricanes: Earth's Mightiest Storms* (Scholastic, 1996)
- Ann McGovern's *Playing with Penguins and Other Adventures in Antarctica* (Scholastic, 1996)
- Wendell Minor's *Grand Canyon: Exploring a Natural Wonder* (Scholastic, 1998)
- Stephen M. Tomecek's *What a Great Idea! Inventions That Changed the World* (Scholastic, 2003)
- Cynthia Rylant's *The Journey: Stories of Migration* (Blue Sky, 2006)
- April Pulley Sayre's *Home at Last: A Song of Migration* (Holt, 1998)
- Diane Siebert's *Mojave* (HarperCollins, 1988) and *Sierra* (HarperCollins, 1991)
- Seymour Simon's *Animal Fact/Animal Fable* (Crown, 1979)
- Peter Sis' *Starry Messenger: Galileo Galilei* (Sunburst, 1996)
- Shelley Tanaka's *On Board the Titanic* (Black Walnut/Madison, 2010)
- Dieter Wiesmuller's *In the Blink of an Eye* (Walker, 2002)
- Alexandra Wright's *Will We Miss Them?* (Charlesbridge, 1992)
- Jane Yolen's *The Ballad of the Pirate Queens* (Harcourt Brace, 1995), *The Mary Celeste* (Aladdin, 2002), and *Roanoke: The Lost Colony* (Simon & Schuster, 2003)
- Nicola Davies' *Bat Loves the Night* (Candlewick, 2004), *One Tiny Turtle* (Candlewick, 2001), and *White Owl, Barn Owl* (Candlewick, 2007)
- Peter and Jean Loewer's *The Moonflower* (Peachtree, 1997)
- Karen Wallace's *Gentle Giant Octopus* (Candlewick, 1998)
- *National Geographic for Kids*
- *Scholastic News*
- *Sports Illustrated for Kids*
- *Ranger Rick*

MATERIALS FOR STUDENTS

Many examples of well-written nonfiction on the same topic. Here is an example text set on Antarctica/Arctic:

- Jennifer Armstrong's *Spirit of Endurance* (Crown, 2000)
- Meredith Hooper's *Antarctic Journal: The Hidden Worlds of Antarctica's Animals* (Frances Lincoln, 2001)
- Alfred Lansing's *Endurance: Shackleton's Incredible Voyage* (Tyndale, 1959)
- Ann McGovern's *Playing with Penguins and Other Adventures in Antarctica* (Scholastic, 1994)
- Diane McKnight's *The Lost Seal* (Moonlight, 2006)
- Debbie S. Miller's *Arctic Lights, Arctic Nights* (Walker, 2003)
- Judy Sierra's *Antarctic Antics: A Book of Penguin Poems* (Gulliver, 1998).

TIME: 45 minutes

Here's How It Goes

One year I was given a copy of *Endurance*, by Alfred Lansing. This is an adult text, but as I read the lead, I was struck by the phenomenal text—how gripping and well written it was. I started bringing it in to show the kids in my classes and they loved it. Here's the lead:

> The whole surface of the ice was a chaos of movement. It looked like an enormous jigsaw puzzle, the pieces stretching away to infinity and being shoved and crunched together by some invisible but irresistible force.

The first time I read this to my students they wanted to find out more, so I found the picture book *Spirit of Endurance*, by Jennifer Armstrong. Now I bring this book to class as well and read the lead, and we discuss how the two leads are different. *Endurance* begins at the most exciting part, when the ship is actually being crushed; *Spirit of Endurance* is written in chronological order so it starts at the beginning. The students love the maps and the photos in both books and are curious to read more. So we read *Spirit of Endurance* cover to cover and they want to know more about Antarctica. They love the writing in this book, too, and want to sketch what they visualize. Here's a sample passage:

Below the equator, seasons are reversed. Although it was November, it was actually spring where Endurance was heading. Shackleton and his crew were hoping for good weather and clear sailing in spite of the Antarctic cold.

Instead, they found ice. As far as the eye could see, there were icebergs and huge, flat fields of sea ice called floes. At the beginning of December, Endurance began picking its way between the bergs, as if finding its way through a maze. (9)

Does that mean you have to do Antarctica? No! Another year our science curriculum emphasized classifying plants and animals, and we studied Colorado animals. The students became fascinated with owls, and I found *The Moon of the Owls*, by Jean Craighead George (HarperCollins Children's, 1993), which prompted us to find several other well-written books on owls. My goal is to demonstrate that you can take one topic and write about it in a myriad of ways.

Another year I began the research unit in October. Because it was close to Halloween, bats seemed to be a great way to bring in nonfiction. *Bat Loves the Night*, by Nicola Davies, got us started, and we looked at facts versus beautiful language. This book is an excellent example of a book that "toggles" back and forth between fiction (story line) and nonfiction (facts). The language in this book (strong, specific verbs and similes) is a wonderful model for crafting well-written nonfiction (see Figure 4.1).

Press Your Advantage

Although I'm bringing in examples of well-written nonfiction and building a repertoire of possibilities for crafting nonfiction, I ask the kids to join the search. Here are the next steps in my "research recipe":

- Read a well-written nonfiction picture book (or an excerpt) a couple times a week. Read feature articles and discuss how well they are written.
- Create a class anchor chart listing the books or excerpts read, along with their characteristics and organizational features. (See the example in Figure 4.2.)

I invite the kids on the search. Why should I do all the work! I ask them to start collecting examples of well-written nonfiction to bring in and share. The

Figure 4.1 Students notice both the facts *and* the author's use of language. The purpose is to demonstrate that nonfiction text should be well written—not boring!

Facts (Nonfiction)	Beautiful Language
Pipistrelle bat	Pixie ears twitch
Finger bones in the wings	Thistledown fur
Body no bigger than thumb	Unfurls
Echolocation–a bat's shout is too high for humans to hear	She beams her voice around her like a flashlight
Babies–batlings	Swoops
Nocturnal	Gliding
Eats dozens of moths in a night or	Fluttering
thousands of tiny gnats, flies, or	Plunges
mosquitoes	Quick as blinking
	Pearly scales are moondust slippery
	Its wings fall like the wrapper from a candy

book baskets in our meeting area quickly fill up with mentor texts, and my students have a wide range of choices by the time they're ready to draft their pieces.

One of my favorite books to start with is *Will We Miss Them?* by Alexandra Wright. There is a brief introduction, followed by discussions of specific animals, the lead for each being "Will we miss the [type of animal]?" After the question are facts about the animal and why the animal is important. Wright ends the book with a conclusion in which she discusses how to help protect animals from extinction. After reading the book to my class, I ask, "Did you like that book? Did you think it was well written?" The answer is unequivocally *yes*. Then I add, "Would you believe that the author was in *sixth grade* when she wrote that?" The light dawns that they, too, can write powerful nonfiction!

As we get closer to drafting, we head to the library with a new purpose. Each student finds two nonfiction books they think are interesting or well written or have great leads. Each student also has two sticky notes with their name on them. They put the sticky notes inside the front cover of the books they've chosen. (The books are checked out under my name; the notes let me know who gets which

Figure 4.2 This is the beginning of an anchor chart that students add to. They notice how nonfiction is organized, and they use what they notice as options when they envision and write their own nonfiction piece.

HOW NONFICTION TEXT IS ORGANIZED

Cow (second person)

- "You" are the cow

- Almost like poetry

- Awesome word choice

- Gave facts (embedded) by following a cow through the day

- Detailed

Will We Miss Them?

- Introduction: "Will we miss them?"

- "Will we miss the _____?" (variety)

- Detailed—at least three facts per animal

- Ending—opinion in it

Gentle Giant Octopus

1. Story—realistic

   - Emotion—you could tell the author cared

   - Sequential

   - Stages of life/birth and how they live

2. Italics—facts

   - Nonfiction

   - Factual/no voice

books.) I want kids to have many books in front of them as we think about crafting our pieces and patterning them after mentor texts.

We use these books in a variety of ways. Sometimes I have each student choose one and share the text organization with the class, and we chart that information (see Figure 4.3). Other times we read through the books and find terrific leads and share them. Students often discover that authors can start with a question or an amazing fact or drop you full force into the setting. We notice what constitutes a great lead—one that captures the reader's attention—and a boring lead—"so and so was born on this date and blah, blah, blah." Another day we may spend our time looking at and labeling how authors end their nonfiction writing (that tends to be hard!).

I give students two weeks to a month to explore topics before they choose one. I want them to pick a topic they are invested in and willing to spend time researching. No grabbing some books at random; topic choice needs to be thoughtful!

When Kids Don't Get It

I eavesdrop and see who truly understands how text is organized and who can't articulate this concept. Students who can't need to revisit this lesson.

One-to-One

Scott has been hesitant to share his thinking, and I want to touch base with him before calling on him to add his book to our class chart.

Me: What nonfiction book are you reading?

Scott: I'm reading about go-carts.

Me: Do you like it?

Scott: Yes, it's really good.

Me: I know you race go-carts, so you must know a lot about them. What makes this book so good?

Scott: Because it gives me new facts.

Me: Tell me about that.

Scott: See how it has pictures. Then it has this box that has lots of information.

Figure 4.3 An extension of our anchor chart (shown in Figure 4.2). This version includes aspects of non-fiction text that can be replicated in student writing. The ideas in the chart also transfer beautifully to the reading workshop and teaching students how to *read* nonfiction text.

ORGANIZATION OF NONFICTION TEXT

- Picture book
- Introduction—questions/answers—conclusion
- Fact/fable or true/false
- Encyclopedia
- Humor with facts embedded
- Diagrams
- Story
- Poetry
- Rhyme
- Alphabet
- Time—sequence—chronological
- Picture/facts
- Comic book
- Photography
- Bold print/italics, etc.
- Glossary
- Table of contents
- Main heading/info
- Newspaper
- First person
- Second person—"you"
- Third person

Me: That's pretty cool. Think about how you could explain to the class how the author did that, and we'll add it to our chart on text organization.

Scott: I'll try.

Owning the Lesson

How often do you present front-loading lessons? In our hurry-up classrooms in which more and more needs to be "covered," time spent lingering as students immerse themselves in books and text features feels like a luxury. What are the benefits? How could this lesson segue into digging into nonfiction texts? How could this lesson transfer to other units of study or to content areas?

Questions to Think About

- In my classroom, who is in charge of noticing how explanatory/informative text is organized?
- Are my students surrounded by a variety of well-written nonfiction texts at a variety of reading levels so that everyone has access to appropriate books?
- Are my students encouraged to model their writing on mentor texts?
- What types of writing are my students doing?
- What skills can I teach using explanatory/informative texts?
- Do my students know how to read nonfiction? Does this transfer to other areas of the curriculum?

Launching an Inquiry Study

Introduction

An inquiry study is quite an undertaking. Before starting, it's important to know your purpose, what you want students to accomplish, and what you want to assess. During this research unit, my students are learning how to:

- Identify and gather sources
- Read and comprehend these sources (informative/explanatory texts)
- Determine the importance of information and take notes
- Ask and answer questions, both literal and inferred
- Think
- Summarize
- Synthesize
- Write
- Speak
- Use technology

In this lesson, I want to catch students' attention and whet their appetites for more. My goal is to tap into their sense of curiosity. So, although this is also an overview, it is the launch into a study.

MENTOR TEXTS FOR TEACHERS

- Harvey Daniels and Steven Zemelman's *Subjects Matter: Every Teacher's Guide to Content-Area Reading* (2004)

- Harvey Daniels, Steven Zemelman, and Nancy Steineke's *Content-Area Writing: Every Teacher's Guide* (Heinemann, 2007)
- Harvey Daniels and Stephanie Harvey's *Comprehension and Collaboration: Inquiry Circles in Action* (Heinemann, 2009)

MENTOR TEXTS FOR STUDENTS

The texts listed in lesson 19 plus:

- Sally Grindley's *Why Is the Sky Blue?* (Anderson, 2006)
- May Garelick's *Where Does the Butterfly Go When It Rains?* (Mondo, 1961); great for showing how asking questions leads to research

MATERIALS FOR STUDENTS

- Picture book that evokes natural curiosity (I love *Why Is the Sky Blue?*)
- Spiral-bound inquiry notebook

TIME: 30 minutes to 1 hour

Here's How It Goes

"At the beginning of the year I asked you to enter our classroom with a sense of wonder, bringing your questions and thinking about things you always wanted to learn about. Today we're going to start a research unit. I want to read this book to you today so that you'll be thinking about all the possibilities."

I read *Why Is the Sky Blue?* and then the students share some of their own questions, wonderings, and topics.

"I'm always researching and taking notes on educators' current ideas about how best to teach. But I'm interested in other things too, and I keep a list of the questions I have or things I want to learn. Today you're going to break in your inquiry notebooks. I'd like you to open them up and let's spend twenty minutes thinking and brainstorming and writing down everything you wonder about or questions you have or topics you're interested in. Then we'll share in groups. Of course, you can keep adding to these lists all year—let's keep them growing!"

Here's Jonny's list:

- D-day
- Scottish wars

▶ **THE NITTY-GRITTY**

Steph Harvey shares a similar strategy for identifying potential topics. If you're looking for even more detail about how to help students identify topics, read her descriptions of Mary Urtz's wonder books on pages 16–22 of *Nonfiction Matters*.

- Vikings
- Hershey
- Sioux Indians
- Ice Age
- Iwo Jima
- Okapi
- Anne Frank
- Holocaust
- Omaha Beach
- Shakespeare
- Mozart
- Trojan War
- Alfred Hitchcock
- JFK
- Olympics

THE LANGUAGE OF LEARNING

I take a very open-ended approach to allowing students to select their own topics. Specifying "umbrella" subjects is another way to go, especially when there is particular content you need to cover. In the past I've had students research some aspect of Colorado history or U.S. history or science or world politics. I just make sure it relates to the curriculum and the standards—that it's not a whim or just "fun."

Jonny is a curious young man with a lot of background knowledge.

But I also see lists like this:

- Dogs
- Horses
- Guinea pigs
- Australia

Press Your Advantage

After generating lists of topics, it's time to trek to the library and start collecting resources. Students today immediately turn to the computer for easy access to information, but I require my students to have *at least* one book for their research. I want them reading! I also want to give students time to discover whether their topic is too broad (World War II, for example, in which case they can narrow it down to something specific about World War II) or too narrow (like the history of earrings; although it's an interesting topic, there's not much out there!).

When Kids Don't Get It

What about the kids who don't wonder about anything, aren't curious? First, the small-group discussions should give them some ideas. I also urge students to go home and visit with their families and talk about potential topics. Before we head to the library, I touch base with the students who need some encouragement. Sometimes it takes awhile to pique their interest.

One-to-One

In the library I notice Kyle wandering without much focus.

Me: So what are you thinking? Any topics or questions?

Kyle: I don't know. Maybe I could get on the computer?

Me: I have another idea. Since we're in the library right now, why don't we walk through the nonfiction section and just look at the titles and topics. Maybe a few will jump out at you.

Kyle: Okay.

Me: Is there a place you want to start? Animals? Space? Places? People? Any specific ideas?

Kyle: I don't know.

Me: Okay, then let's start at the beginning. [*We head to nonfiction and start reading titles and talking about potential topics. When one piques Kyle's interest, we pull books out. When we're done, Kyle has books on grizzly bears and snakes*.]

Kyle: I don't know which one I want to do.

Me: That's okay, we have time. Why don't you check out a book on each and spend the next week reading them both and decide which topic interests you more right now.

Kyle: I could do that.

He finally settles on grizzly bears.

▶ THE NITTY-GRITTY

How long you allow students to gather and explore texts is up to you and depends on the previous exposure and practice students have had with explanatory/informative text and the research process. How much explicit instruction do your students need? What is their background knowledge with regard to nonfiction? How much time *can* you allow? If doing research is something totally new, I allow two weeks to a month. But during that time students are also learning how to read nonfiction text and take notes. I'm laying the foundation for independent work. If students have done a research project before, I shorten the immersion period to one or two weeks.

Owning the Lesson

Who chooses the topics, you or your students? What is your *purpose*? Is it to focus on a time period or theme in history? Is it to work on science? Even when you identify an umbrella topic, students still have choice and ownership and thus buy-in. Are students preparing to write reports or learning to be researchers? Is this an authentic task leading to information they will use for the rest of their lives? How can you bring aspects of this lesson into your own classroom to meet your students' needs and your curricular objectives?

Questions to Think About

- Who is in charge of picking topics? What kind of guidance do my students receive?

- How much time do my students need to choose topics they're truly invested in and will stick with over a long period of time?

- Do I give my students opportunities to gather texts and materials?

- Do I foster a sense of wonder and curiosity in the classroom?

- How will students' exposure to their classmates' research expand the curriculum?

Making Expectations Explicit

Introduction

Before we start our formal research, I give students a packet that includes a timeline, deadlines, expectations, and a contract. I explain each component. Experience has taught me this is integral to students' time management and long-term planning. Not all research projects need to be this elaborate. Use my expectations as a guideline. Pull out elements appropriate to your classroom.

MENTOR TEXTS FOR TEACHERS

- Harvey Daniels and Stephanie Harvey's *Comprehension and Collaboration: Inquiry Circles in Action* (2009)

MATERIALS FOR STUDENTS

- All the mentor texts they've gathered
- Resources they've collected on their topic
- Packet of expectations (deadlines, guidelines, contract)

TIME: 30 minutes

Here's How It Goes

"I have had so much fun watching and listening to you learn and talk about your research topics. I think most of you have settled on your topic. Before we go any further, why don't we do a quick status check and share our topics." Students share.

"Now it's time to get to work and start taking notes. My former students have helped me teach better by giving feedback on this unit, and they really wanted deadlines; they also wanted to see the whole picture and all the pieces. So I've laid it all out for you. We're going to go over it and discuss it now, and then you're going to take this home and explain it to your parents. You might want to put the page of deadlines on the refrigerator, and you need to have the contract signed by a parent or guardian. That way I'll know that they know what I expect from you." We read and discuss the packet, so that we're all on the same page.

I wrote the contract Steph Harvey includes in *Nonfiction Matters* (see pages 193–95) in 1998, and I still use something similar. I change it a bit every year, though. The letter in Figure 4.4 is leaner. (Figure 4.5 spells out the requirements and functions as a timeline/contract.) I've also built in more opportunities to tie in technology because technology keeps advancing. Nevertheless, the benefits of a research project are as powerful now as they were ten years ago!

Press Your Advantage

This is where differentiation and knowing your students comes in. For example, if you have students who need the requirements adapted, change up the contracts. Pull in technology. Bring in experts. Each year I tweak the process to fit the kids in my class.

When Kids Don't Get It

A research project like this goes most smoothly when there is a strong home–school connection. The reality today is that sometimes that connection is hard to establish. For some students, support at home is negligible. I expect every student to return a signed contract. In some cases, that means I need to contact the parents myself. I also need to be aware which students need additional support at school to complete this research unit successfully and give them that support.

Figure 4.4 An example of a letter I would write to my students (and parents!) to introduce a research project and to make expectations clear.

January 7, 2011

Dear Students,

During the month of December, we began to investigate topics and collect resources for our research project. Now you've committed to your topic and started taking notes! I'm excited to see what you learn, and I'm looking forward to researching with you.

I will teach you the research process as we go, but this is *your* project. Most of the work will be done at school, but you also need to read and take notes at home. I encourage you to ask your parents to help you manage your time. This is our first long-term project, so it's broken down by sections, with a due date for each section. These are attached, and I suggest you post them at home where you can't miss them!

You'll be spending most of January taking three-column notes in your inquiry notebook. You will also need to keep track of all your resources for a bibliography. Then we will draft our nonfiction piece *in class*. Once your rough draft is complete, you may take it home to finalize, but *both the rough draft and final draft need to be turned in*. At the end of February or the beginning of March, you'll give a five- to fifteen-minute presentation to the class on your topic.

We're going to learn so much from one another! I hope you've picked a topic you're genuinely interested in and will have fun working on for two months!

Sincerely,

Mrs. Blauman

Figure 4.5 My expectations for students. This allows them to see the "big picture," while breaking the process into manageable pieces. The signature section is critical to communicate with parents and to provide accountability.

RESEARCH REQUIREMENTS
Second Trimester

NOTES
You will be taking three-column notes in your inquiry notebook. These will be organized around a minimum of five (5) questions on your topic.

BIBLIOGRAPHY
Make sure you record *all* your resources, as you will include a bibliography in your report. Your bibliography will be a page separate from your feature article. You may use *Noodletools* to format your bibliography. (You should record your resources in the third column of your notes.)

ROUGH DRAFT
You will write a rough draft of a nonfiction text in class. We will be studying the many ways to write nonfiction, and you will need to choose a mentor piece to use as a model.

FINAL DRAFT
You will finalize your rough draft at home. Final drafts need to be typed or written in ink. Your rough draft *must* be turned in with your final draft.

PRESENTATION
You will give an oral presentation to the class about your topic. This can be from five to fifteen minutes long. It helps to practice at home and to use note cards. You may *not* read your report, however. You will also need a *visual aid* during your presentation. This could be a poster, a model, anything that will enhance your presentation.

RESEARCH TIMELINE

January 16–February 20	Note taking
February 23–March 18	Drafting
March 18	Rough draft due
March 18–March 25	Finalizing and practicing presentations
March 23–March 27	Classroom presentations
March 26	Rough draft and final draft due

DUE DATES

Notes	February 20
Rough draft	March 18
Presentations	March 23–March 27
Final draft	March 26
(rough draft must be turned in, too!)	

RESEARCH CONTRACT
Please return this form by January 14

Name _____   Topic _____

I have read the requirements, timeline, due dates, etc.

Student Signature:

_____

Parent Signature:

_____

One-to-One

Although Heather is using class time well, it's taken her quite a while to return her signed contract. Because completing homework in general is tough for Heather, we need to come up with a plan/solution.

Me: Thanks for getting your contract back signed. Have you been having fun reading about hamsters?

Heather: I have the book from the school library that I've been reading.

Me: Have you gotten any other books?

Heather: No, Mom is at work, so we can't go anywhere.

Me: I understand. Sometimes it's hard to get things done at night, isn't it?

Heather: Yeah, because I have to watch my little brother.

Me: I want you to be honest—are you reading thirty minutes at night, though?

Heather: Most of the time, yeah. As long as I can understand the book. If it's too hard, I quit.

Me: Thanks for being straight with me. I'm thinking maybe we need to work something out so that you can get some more reading and note taking done here at school with me. What do you think?

Heather: I think that would help.

We all have different structures in place for working with kids who need "more." Before school or after school? That often depends on student transportation. Lunch and recess? I'm reluctant to take break time away from kids, but sometimes it's the only option—and if Heather and I spend a working lunch together and get more reading/note taking done, that helps her and probably needn't be viewed negatively. I grapple with these tough issues all the time, but Heather needs to be successful, and I need to be there to support her, even if it's just spending a little extra time with her. If the majority of my class needs this kind of support, then I need to build the majority of the research work into our class time.

Owning the Lesson

What expectations do you have for your students? What is the timeline, what are the deadlines? It's imperative to think through this unit of study before you start so that the students see both the big picture and all the smaller elements that are part of completing the process and producing the product. How much independence do you want to give your students? Will the bulk of the work be completed at home or at school? What background knowledge do students have when they begin this project? How much scaffolding will they need to be successful? How do you include parents/family?

Questions to Think About

- What are my goals for a research unit of study? Are they broken down into manageable parts?

- How do I communicate expectations and deadlines to both students and parents?

- Have I provided direct instruction in and modeled all the components of the research process? Who owns the process?

- Is there a support system in place for students who don't have support at home?

- How does this unit teach long-range planning and encourage stamina?

- Is this an authentic use of class time? Will students use the research process?

- How much choice do students have? Enough for them to buy in to the task?

Becoming Experts

Introduction

Students now need to commit to their topic, tightening their focus and narrowing the topic if necessary. Becoming an expert on a topic also includes time to linger and collect resources—books, magazines, articles, links to Internet material, primary sources, and so on.

MENTOR TEXTS FOR STUDENTS
The mentor texts listed for lesson 19 work beautifully for this lesson, as well.

MATERIALS FOR STUDENTS
- Inquiry notebook
- Books, magazines, Internet connection, other resources

TIME: 2 weeks to a month

Here's How It Goes

"Today we're heading to the library to continue to gather resources on our possible topics. I know you guys love going to the library because it allows us to spread out. We're going to the library every Tuesday for the next couple of weeks to check out books, use the computers, and read, read, read. Remember, no notes yet.

"You have a couple of options for how you use your time in the library. You could look for books and check them out; order books from other libraries in the district; read; or use a computer to search the Internet (if you do that, remember to write down the site in your inquiry notebook, so you can go back to it later). I'm not going to do a status check, but do let me know if you need help or a conference. I'll make sure I'll get to you first."

We head to the library, where students dig into the resources. I work with students who've asked for help, confer, and check in.

Pressing Your Advantage

As students solidify their topic choices, I give them colored sentence strips on which they write their name and their topic, which they then post on the bulletin board (under a banner like In the Know or Ask the Experts or What We're Researching). If classmates find resources related to another student's topic or have ideas about potential people for someone else to interview, they write their suggestion on a sticky note and attach it to the appropriate sentence strip. For example, Lindsay's uncle worked with the seals at the Denver Zoo. When she saw that another student was researching seals, she left a note saying, "See me—I can help set up an interview." Another student flagged an upcoming Discovery special dealing with a classmate's topic.

When Kids Don't Get It

Some students continually change topics. One week it's the Broncos, the next week it's the history of baseball, then on to something else. At some point I have to put my foot down. When the deadline finally arrives, the rubber hits the road. Students need to make their choice and *stick to it*. The research process is different from that of writing a story; there needs to be commitment and follow-through. That's why I allow so much time for immersion—so students make thoughtful choices and own those decisions.

▶ **THE NITTY-GRITTY**

Why no notes? The bottom line is reading comprehension. To ask deep, thoughtful questions, students need strong background knowledge. I want my students to focus on becoming knowledgeable about their topic so that when it's time to ask "thick" questions, they have a lot to draw on. Questions created to guide research *before* students are conversant with their topic are formulaic, forced, and shallow. Then, too, students are still deciding whether this is the topic they want to follow through on. The purpose here is for them to immerse themselves in learning and move toward commitment. *Then* it's time to take notes!

▶ **THE NITTY-GRITTY**

Stephanie Harvey nudged me to extend the concept of collecting material beyond books to things like magazines and maps (see page 15 of *Nonfiction Matters*). My students ran with the idea, and it was Lindsay who first suggested an interview as a source of information. Classroom collaboration!

One-to-One

Erin realizes she might have problems committing to her topic and requests a conference.

Erin: Mrs. B, I really wanted to learn about the history of earrings, but I only found like a paragraph when I looked online. And there are no books on it.

Me: Right. Sometimes we have phenomenal questions, but the answers are short or there's just not any information. So what now?

Erin: Well, I looked into the history of jewelry. But that's really hard to find info on, too.

Me: That doesn't surprise me. But we need to talk about time management. You've been looking for a couple weeks, and next week you have to make a final decision. I want you to have enough time to collect some resources and read a bit before we start taking notes. You've got to find a topic that you can stick with. What are you thinking?

Erin: Can I have today to look some more and then come back to you and make a final decision?

Me: Absolutely. Do you have a couple ideas, though, before I send you off?

Erin: Actually, I do. I think I want to find out about frogs and toads because I want to buy one and I don't know which to choose.

Me: That works. Tell me what you decide before we head back to class!

Owning the Lesson

Have you acknowledged the power of lingering and allowing students the time to read and build background knowledge—to solidify their interest in their topic, commit to it, and learn about it without having to worry about notes? How much time do your students need? How much time did your research projects take when you were a student? What might you take from that experience and embed into your process?

It's worth the time spent allowing students to build background knowledge before launching into notes. While students are reading and immersing themselves in their topics (both in reading workshop and in writing workshop) it is an opportune time to teach or review note taking, being explicit about what it entails. Then, when students begin taking notes, they have the skills they need to work independently and successfully.

Questions to Think About

- Why is time such an important part of this lesson?
- How much time do my students need to immerse themselves in their topic? How much time can I allot to this?
- How does this lesson solidify student choice?
- How does this lesson encourage deeper understanding of a topic?
- How does the importance of background knowledge apply across the curriculum?

Asking Questions
to Guide Research

Introduction

Once students have committed to a topic, they need to ask the questions that will frame their research and drive their notes. Quality questions are imperative for successful research.

MENTOR TEXT FOR STUDENTS

- Kathy Wollard's *How Come? Planet Earth*, part of the How Come? series (Workman, 1999)

MATERIALS FOR STUDENTS

- Inquiry notebook

TIME: 45 minutes to an hour

Here's How It Goes

"Now that you've been reading about your topic and becoming familiar with it, it's time to prepare to take notes. Today we're going to ask the thick questions that will frame our notes. Does anyone think they know why I've let you spend so much time reading and gaining background knowledge before we start asking our questions?"

The kids think for a bit, and then Rachael's hand shoots up. "It's the hook! The hook you always say we have to have to hang new learning on! We had to know about our topic first."

THE LANGUAGE OF LEARNING

One of the best books I've read on content reading is *Subjects Matter: Every Teacher's Guide to Content-Area Reading*, by Harvey Daniels and Steven Zemelman (2004). They make such a powerful argument for building background knowledge for our students:

> The ability to get meaning from print is dependent on what we already know. Those same brain scientists believe that the only way we can learn new information is by attaching it, connecting it, and integrating it with information we already have. You have to assimilate the information into an existing schema or revise an old one to make the new stuff fit. Either way, you have to work with what is already in the mind; you can't build on nothing. (27)

They also talk about giving our students hooks to hang new thinking on. So powerful! I share my reading and learning with my students. When I shared that idea of the hook, it caught on. When we make the abstract concrete, students understand.

"Rachael, you definitely understand about that hook! Background knowledge gets us deeper, doesn't it? We've worked so hard on asking questions and I think you all know that you ask rich, deep questions when you read. Now we're going to ask deep questions about our topics. A couple weeks ago, you might not have been able to do that.

"I'm going to throw a couple of questions at you and I want you to tell me if they're thick or thin questions. What year did the Oscars start?"

That's Cooper's topic. He answers, "Oh, that's thin. I can answer that in one sentence."

"Okay, let's try another. Why was Cleopatra such a powerful queen?"

Lucie answers. "Thick. If I ask that question I'm going to get a lot of information. Can I use that one?"

"Sure. I could keep going like this, but the point I'm making is that your questions have to be thick—that way you'll find out lots of information. And you'll need at least five thick questions to research, because you'll have to write a minimum of five paragraphs."

Dexter's hand is up already. "Mrs. B., I want to take notes on just some facts besides answering my questions. Can I do that?"

"Do you see fact sections in the nonfiction books you read?"

"Yes."

"Then I suggest that when you set up your notes you create a section for 'fast facts' or extra interesting information. Would that work?" He nods.

"What if I don't find answers to all my questions?" worries Emma.

"What could you do?" I ask.

"If I can't find answers to a question, can I just add another?"

"I think that would be a great strategy. In fact, you can continue to add questions any time as you research and take notes."

I answer any remaining questions and then send the students off to talk with a partner about some possible questions, get feedback, and ask their partner to suggest some questions on their topic. Then students return to their table, write a minimum of five thick questions in their inquiry notebooks, and turn those questions in to me to okay. Figure 4.6 is a list of questions from a student's inquiry notebook.

Figure 4.6 Notice the range and depth of questions included here. While Reed needs one more question, this is a great start. These are all student-generated. How does that compare to teacher-generated?

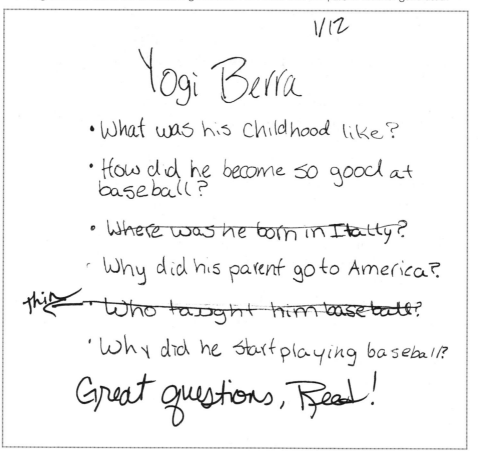

Pressing Your Advantage

I read over all the notebooks and check the questions. I'm serious when I expect a minimum of five *thick* questions. If a student has that, I give them the okay. If a student has written thin questions, I make sure I confer with him or her the next day.

When Kids Don't Get It

Generally there are a handful of students who have written thin questions or questions that reveal they have a limited understanding of their topic. I pull them together in a group and we co-construct thicker questions.

One-to-One

Kate has more than five questions, but I notice they're mostly thin or won't require much research.

Me: Can we take a look at the questions you wrote yesterday? I'd like to talk about which ones you think are thick and that you can get a lot of information on and which ones might be thin. You like the topic of Amelia Earhart, don't you?

Kate: I think she's great. I know so much already. [*She recounts some of what she knows.*]

Me: Whew! That is a lot. But let's think about all you know and revisit your questions. How about this first one: *Did she have any brothers or sisters?* Can you answer that?

Kate: Yes. I see—I can answer that in a couple words. That's thin.

Me: That's what I wanted you to notice. Read through the rest of your questions. What do you notice?

Kate: A lot of them are thin. How do I change them?

Me: Well, you've asked about her family and if she got to fly when she was a kid. How about making it a bigger investigation like *What was her childhood like?* Then you could take notes on stuff she did when she was a kid.

Kate: I think I understand. So I could ask a question like *What did she have to do to learn how to fly?* instead of *What year did she fly for the first time?*

Me: Perfect. Want to have another go and then let me check those notes?

Kate is already at work and simply nods.

Owning the Lesson

So often when students write reports, the teacher sets the questions or the headings. Think of the old "state reports" standby: population, size, history, economy, and so on. Asking deep, thick, thoughtful questions puts the student in charge. They own the research. But you are there to guide. Asking questions is an important skill—in all areas of the curriculum and in life. Think about previous research projects or reports your students have produced in your classroom. How is this lesson similar or different? How can you transfer the comprehension strategy of asking questions to writing a research article?

Questions to Think About

- In my classroom who creates the questions that frame each individual research project?

- Do my students know how to create thick questions– ones that move them to deeper and more meaningful information on their topic?

- How does asking thick questions transfer to other areas of my curriculum?

- How do thick questions lead to better research and deeper understanding of a topic?

Lesson 24

Determining Importance of Ideas in Text

Introduction

The majority of the nonfiction reading we do in my classroom comes from articles and supplementary texts, not textbooks. With the accessibility of the Internet and the speed with which technology grows, nonfiction articles are literally at our fingertips. Also, as more classrooms begin to incorporate interactive systems like SMART Boards, the ability to pull text up on a screen and highlight it, revise it, add to it, and move it lets us introduce a wide array of teaching strategies. Once students know how to mark text to hold their thinking about it, they can do it anywhere.

But I also want to bring in text for the kids to read and work from. The books in Kathy Wollard's How Come? series (Workman) are filled with well-written fun-to-read information on a variety of science and social studies subjects. Even better, the questions are all kid-generated. These types of articles lead directly to note taking, and note-taking techniques can then be applied to the textbook.

When I choose an article to work with the class, I like to connect it to the curriculum. Below I use "Why Does a Porcupine Have Quills? How Do They Work?," a chapter in *How Come? Planet Earth*, as a model. Reason one, I've told the story of Bandit and the porcupine the week I was interviewed as president of the class, and reason two, porcupines are indigenous to Colorado, so it's related to our study of Colorado plants and animals. Any nonfiction article could be used here, as long as it's well written and it causes students to think.

MENTOR TEXT FOR TEACHERS

- Harvey Daniels and Nancy Steineke's *Texts and Lessons for Content-Area Reading* (2011)

MENTOR TEXT FOR STUDENTS

- Kathy Wollard's *How Come? Planet Earth* from the How Come? series (Workman, 1993)

MATERIALS

- Copies of a well-written nonfiction article, one for each student
- Pencils and highlighters
- Document camera or overhead projector

TIME: 1 hour

Here's How It Goes

"We've looked at how textbooks are organized, but I think nonfiction articles are sometimes harder to read, because they don't have a key to unlock them the way a textbook does. You have to read nonfiction a little differently, and often you have to decide what's important to remember. This article is from a terrific book called *How Come? Planet Earth*, which I love because every article starts with a question that establishes the purpose; the book is well written and fun to read; and most importantly, all the questions it answers came from kids." I pass out the article.

"Before we start reading, let's survey the article and the organization." We look at the two pages and notice that there are no headings or similar clues that we normally see in a textbook. "Now let's look at the title, which is a question. Good readers ask questions *before*, *during*, and *after* reading, so I want you to use your background knowledge and jot down what you think the answer to this question is. In the white space above the title, write *Before* and then leave tracks in the snow about what you the think the answer is." After students complete this step we discuss their answers, which helps focus the lesson and provide a purpose—to see whether they were correct.

"Because this is our first go at an article like this, I'm going to model my thinking first, and then turn the work over to you halfway through. We're going to highlight the text that answers the specific question. We'll also be pulling the main ideas out of the paragraphs."

We read the first paragraph together, deciding what to highlight and jotting notes in the margin about the main idea. I model on the document camera as each student marks her or his paper. After we've done a couple paragraphs together, I say, "Okay, now let's see how our thinking matches. We'll read this next paragraph together and then I'm going to turn off the camera and highlight what's important while you mark your paper. Then I'll turn it back on and we'll compare what we did." After this scaffold, students finish the final paragraphs with a partner.

Then I ask for one more set of tracks in the snow. "At the bottom of the last page, I'd like you to write *After* and answer the question in the title again. How many of you have changed your thinking since you've read the article? It's okay to lift words and phrases from the text; in fact, that's a great strategy. Let's do that now."

To finish, table groups share and discuss their final answers. We also discuss that all answers should be in the same ballpark because the text *literally* answers the question.

CCSS, GRADE BY GRADE

All the reading standards for informational text are addressed in lessons 23, 24, and 25. Here I'm focusing on the first two informational reading standards in each grade.

Third graders ask and answer questions to demonstrate an understanding of the text (the answers refer explicitly to the text). They also determine the main idea of a text and recount the key details. *Lesson 23 supports asking questions; in this lesson and throughout the research process students determine the main idea and details from their reading.*

Fourth graders refer to details and examples in a text when explaining what the text says explicitly and when drawing inferences from the text. They also determine the main idea supported by key details and summarize the text. *This lesson shows students how to determine importance and the main idea; as students work on their notes (lesson 25), they use both explicit and inferred information.*

Fifth graders quote accurately from a text when explaining what the text says explicitly and when drawing from the text. They also determine two or more main ideas supported by key details and summarize the text. *Students who are able to highlight the important details in text can use those to quote from it accurately.*

Sixth graders cite textual evidence to support their analysis of what the text says explicitly as well as what they infer. They determine a central idea of the text and how it is conveyed through particular details and summaries of the text. *These skills are addressed in this lesson and lesson 25.*

Pressing Your Advantage

I continue to work with my students on determining importance in nonfiction articles until I feel they understand and are ready to take notes. Lesson options include:

- Highlight what's important in one color and what's interesting in another.

- Have students read the article, record facts and interesting information on sticky notes, place the notes on charts at the front of the room labeled *Important* and *Interesting*, and compare and discuss.

- Summarize *Time for Kids* feature articles in the "Connections— Constructed Response" section of the book lover's book.

- Create an anchor chart listing what students notice about determining importance in nonfiction text. (See the example in Figure 4.7.)

TO LEARN MORE

Stephanie Harvey goes into great detail on the difference between what's important and what's interesting beginning on page 82 of *Nonfiction Matters*.

When Kids Don't Get It

Working with all students on the same piece of text is "one size fits all." When I ask students to work through articles independently and some students find it too difficult, I pull together a guided reading group of kids who need support.

One-to-One

The students are reading an article on why leaves change colors. I notice that Heather is having difficulty.

Me: Let's read this article together and decide what we should highlight as important. I see you've already made your predictions about the answer to the question.

Heather: I think it's because it turns cold. Leaves turn color in the fall when it gets cold.

Me: That makes sense. Now, as we read this together, see whether your thinking changes. It's your job to decide what is important—what information in the text answers this question. Will you read the first paragraph out loud for me? [*Heather reads*.] Tell me what you think that paragraph is about.

Heather: It kind of talks about all the colors that leaves turn in the fall.

Me: You're right, it does. Is there anything in that paragraph that answers the question?

Figure 4.7 An example of a co-constructed anchor chart. Students created this list.

CUES/WAYS TO DETERMINE IMPORTANCE IN NONFICTION

- Titles and headings

- Subtitles

- Text changes/color

- Highlighting

- Bold/italics

- Underlining

- Pictures, captions, maps

- Focus questions

- Gist (fun facts)

- Pronunciation keys

- Graphs, timelines

- Index

- Glossary

- Table of Contents

- Titles

Heather: Not really.

Me: As your writing teacher I want you to notice that—sometimes the author will write a paragraph that's a lead, that kind of sets the whole thing up. Shall we keep going?

And we do. We read paragraph by paragraph, highlighting and discussing the main idea in each. At the end, I have Heather write a paragraph summarizing what she learned from the text.

Owning the Lesson

Is this a one-time lesson or one that needs to be repeated and reinforced? Is it a reading lesson or a writing lesson or both? How does it prepare students for taking notes? How often do you bring informative and explanatory text into your classroom? Often enough to be sure students know how to read it strategically? When learning to determine importance in text, students often need a lot of time and practice with a variety of texts at different levels of difficulty.

This lesson could be taught during a research study or any time during the year when students need instruction on determining importance in text and learning to read nonfiction. Using it earlier in the year could scaffold later research work. It could also be incorporated into science, social studies, math, and so on.

Questions to Think About

- How do I teach so that my students know how to determine importance in text independently? How do I support my students who aren't ready to take notes independently?

- How often do I explicitly teach my students that background knowledge informs their knowledge of a topic *before* they begin reading and that their thinking changes *during* reading and *after* reading?

- Do my students have opportunities to determine what is important in text and what is interesting to them and how sometimes the two overlap? How do they demonstrate this?

- Could I transfer this lesson to a variety of explanatory/informative texts, not just textbooks?

- Could I use this lesson to teach note taking?

Developing Voice While Taking Notes

Introduction

This lesson builds on lesson 1, which teaches students to take two-column notes for president paragraphs. Taking three-column notes is a natural extension. In the lesson I hand out copies of "What Makes Hail?" from *How Come?* and ask students to write down at the top of their paper what they *think* the answer to the question is. The lesson is identical to the lesson on determining importance in text, except instead of highlighting and leaving tracks in the snow, students record their notes and thinking in the three-column format.

MENTOR TEXT FOR STUDENTS
- Kathy Wollard's *How Come? Planet Earth* from the How Come? series (Workman, 1993)

MATERIALS FOR STUDENTS
- Copy of a nonfiction article
- Inquiry notebook

TIME: 1 hour

Here's How It Goes

I have on the board two pieces of chart paper adjoining each other, ready to start a new anchor chart.

"Okay, you guys are awesome at determining importance in nonfiction text, and you're terrific at taking notes when you interview the president of the week. Today we're going to combine these skills and learn how to take notes on articles. After we practice a bit, I'll expect you to take notes on your content reading in science and social studies. Remember, I'm always trying to teach you the way adults would be taught, and taking notes like this is something college students do. Think how prepared you'll be!

"I've divided one piece of chart paper like we do when we take notes for our president paragraphs—two columns, *main idea* and *details*. But I've drawn a spiral between the two pieces of chart paper to show that the third column is going to be one whole page of the two-page spread when you open your spiral notebook. That third column is going to be where you write down your *thinking* —your con- nections and questions and lingering thoughts. That third column is also the place to record what's really interesting to you and *why*. Let's try it with this article. I'll start, then I'm going to ask you to help me." (See Figure 4.8.)

Press Your Advantage

Students apply this note-taking technique to their research by writing a research question across the top of a two-page spread in their notebook and constructing the three columns. If they need more space, they use another two-page spread.

The third column is the toughest one for the kids to complete, so we read another article together. This time I give each student three sticky notes and ask them to write down three questions, connections, speculations, or any other thoughts they have as we're working through the piece. When we've completed the reading and entered the main ideas and details on the anchor chart, students place their sticky notes in the third column across from the appropriate main idea. This highlights the variety of thinking that occurs.

The third column is where the note taker's voice emerges. The third column pushes students to summarize and synthesize and pursue their own investiga- tions. The third column shows students' interaction with and thinking about the text—and that's what comprehension is all about! (See Figure 4.9.)

Figure 4.8 This chart became an anchor text example for the class for how to take three-column notes. It is also an example of gradual release—I started by modeling, but the comment in the third column about wind strength came from the students.

Main Idea	Details	Deeper Thinking (connections, questions, speculations, etc.)
Dangerous/ damage	Punch holes in plane wings Kills horses, cows, animals Creates rushing rainwater–6 ft. drifts of hail Destroy crops (broken stems)	Didn't know that! How many people have died from hail?
Forms of hail	In thunderstorms ice freezes around blowing particles–dust, debris, bugs! Layers of ice Milky layers = colder temp Clear layers = warmer temp Strong winds in the clouds (180 mph)	Wow! 90 mph winds are strong, imagine 180 mph! Like a hurricane!
Thunderclouds (height)	50% chance of hail– 8 miles 75% chance of hail– 9 miles 100% chance of hail– 11 miles	

Figure 4.9 Sydney's notes show her understanding about swans and her thinking and connections in the third column.

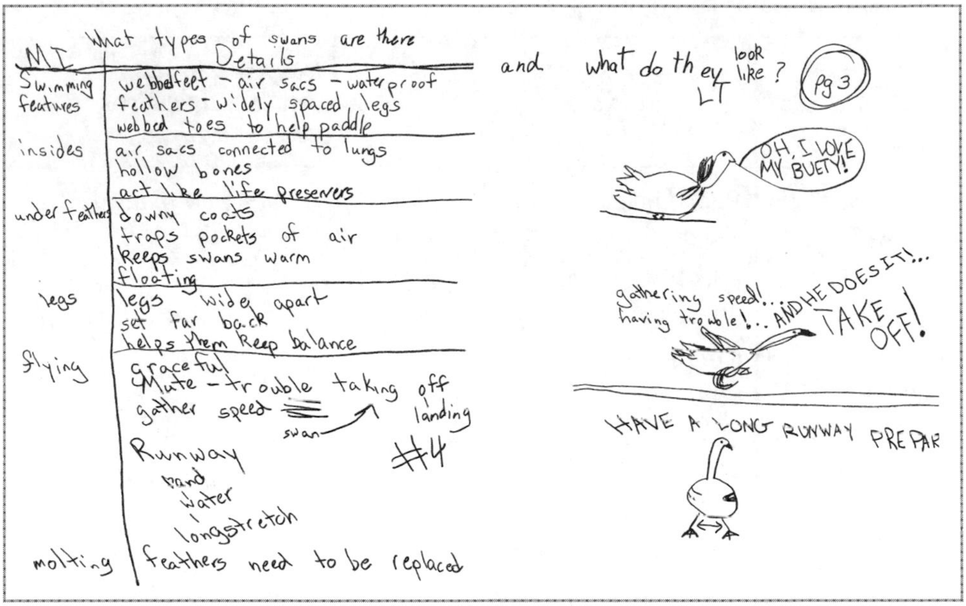

When Kids Don't Get It

This is a model lesson; I co-construct with the students. As we continue to practice and I release responsibility to the students, it becomes obvious which students need support. I either pull them together in a group for explicit instruction or give them text at their reading level.

One-to-One

Brett has been hard at work, but he hasn't written anything in the third column.

Me: You're doing a phenomenal job in the first two columns of your notes but it looks like maybe the third column is tough for you. Tell me about that.

Brett: Sometimes I just don't have any questions or connections. I read it and that's all.

Me: That happens. But sometimes what you read makes you ask more questions. Or makes you wonder. I can only tell that you're interacting with the text and thinking at a deeper level from your notes in the third column. What do you think we could do to practice that?

Brett: You really want me to do this?

Me: What do you think?

Brett: Yeah. I guess you do. Maybe when we do another *Time for Kids* article I'll work on that third column and show you my thinking?

Me: How about telling me what you're thinking right now, so that you can get something written in that third column and see that it's not that tough. I appreciate that you want to try it in another *Time for Kids* article, and I can't wait to hear about your thinking on that, but let's try it right now while I'm sitting here.

With that, Brett continues to talk about his thinking and we add that to his third column. I find that students can *talk* about their thinking, but often have difficulty transferring that to writing it down in the third column.

Owning the Lesson

What could you take from this lesson and use in your classroom? How do you want your students to take notes? How do you want them to organize their notes? When I was in school we used five-by-seven-inch note cards with questions or topics written across the top. I'd lose them, or they didn't have enough space. But they work for some, and if they work for you and your students use them, absolutely.

I use the three-column note format because I emphasize the thinking and interaction with text that the third column captures (there's not enough space to do that on a note card). Students take their notes in their spiral-bound inquiry notebook, but they also keep a research folder for articles, Internet printouts, and so on.

Questions to Think About

- Have my students taken notes before?
- How will my students organize their notes? Where will they keep them?
- Am I in charge of creating questions or topics for notes, or are my students?
- How often do I check my students' notes for progress?
- How long will my students be taking notes?
- What about my students who still cannot take notes independently? How can I ensure their success?
- Will my students take notes at school or at home or both? What about students who have little or no support at home?

Envisioning Texts

Introduction

Katie Wood Ray writes extensively about teaching students to envision how their writing is going to look when it's complete. What other published works will it resemble? Instead of saying, "I'm going to write about owls," a child needs to be specific and explain what her piece will look like: "I'm going to write a question-and-answer book about owls and I'm going to add pictures."

Envisioning is the first step in crafting. By this point, the students have been exposed to so many different types of nonfiction that they have a wide array from which to choose. My Learning Disability students (on IEPs) or English as a second language students may need explicit guidance, but everyone can create a piece of nonfiction (ABC books are great choices for students learning English).

MENTOR TEXTS FOR STUDENTS

Your room should already be bursting with nonfiction texts, but send your students to the library to search for more!

MATERIALS FOR STUDENTS

- A nonfiction mentor text
- Inquiry notebook

TIME: 45 minutes

Here's How It Goes

I have students identify the piece they're using as an example or mentor text and write a paragraph explaining how they envision their piece will look. I ask them to tell me whether it will be written in first person, second person, or third person and to include any other nonfiction text features they are planning to add—glossary, important facts, maps, pictures and captions, and so on. (I've never had a child use a textbook as a mentor piece!) See Figure 4.10 for an example.

Figure 4.10 Jonah writes about how he envisions his research piece will look. He's modeling this after books he read while he took notes.

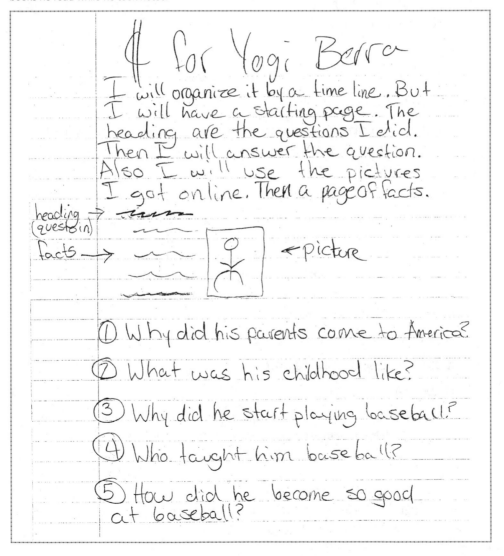

Press Your Advantage

I collect these paragraphs, read them, and return them the following day with my comments. Knowing exactly what my students are working on helps me confer more effectively.

When Kids Don't Get It

From these paragraphs I also know who doesn't have a mentor text and who isn't envisioning what the final product will look like. I share examples of published texts appropriate for their topic with these students, and we discuss what their final piece should look like.

One-to-One

After reading Oscar's paragraph, I know I need to have a conference!

> **Me:** I read your paragraph about how you see your piece turning out, and it wasn't clear to me. Could you show me a book you're using as a mentor text? That would help me understand.
>
> **Oscar:** I want to write about Mexico. I know about Mexico.
>
> **Me:** Yes, you know a lot about it, because you go back often to visit. But if I were to ask you to find a book that yours would look like, can you show me one? [*Oscar thinks for a minute and says he's not sure.*] When I conferred with you and we looked at your questions, I thought that your information reminds me of a book that tells the reader the best parts of a state or country or geographical area. These are called *guidebooks*. What do you think?
>
> **Oscar:** That's kind of what I've been doing.
>
> **Me:** Have you seen books like that?
>
> **Oscar:** No.
>
> **Me:** How about I bring in a couple I have at home and we'll see whether they match what you're thinking. If they don't, then we'll find something else.
>
> **Oscar:** Okay.

Sometimes the answer isn't clear-cut and we have to work at it. But I always want my students to have some choice and control over their writing.

Owning the Lesson

How is this lesson different from asking students to write five-paragraph themes or a traditional report on one of the United States? Who chooses and owns what the final piece will look like? In this lesson students are writing nonfiction pieces (often feature articles) modeled on published examples. They could also be writing persuasive pieces.

What are your goals for student writing? What is your purpose? What type of piece do you want students to write? Do you want structured reports or something different? The format needs to be explicit, and students need an abundance of models and mentor texts at their fingertips. Even when you have chosen the format, they still need to articulate how they envision their final piece.

Questions to Think About

- Once my students have chosen a topic, can they envision and explain what their final piece will look like? What they are modeling their writing on?

- How do previous lessons scaffold the idea of using mentor texts to envision the product?

- How do my students choose mentor texts? How can I ensure that there is a wide variety of nonfiction texts in my classroom to guide their writing?

- How do the preceding lessons in this cluster scaffold this lesson, lay the foundation for it?

- What if a student's original vision isn't working? How do I help him or her change direction or change mentor texts?

- What will I do if a student wants to change the topic after or while writing his or her draft?

Using Paragraphs Effectively

Introduction

Paragraphing is a sophisticated skill. Although we've worked on narrative and descriptive paragraphing in other lessons, my objective here is for students to notice how published nonfiction authors create authentic paragraphs and the rules they follow and to transfer this knowledge to their own nonfiction writing.

MENTOR TEXT FOR STUDENTS

- Jennifer Armstrong's *Spirit of Endurance* (Crown, 2000), any other text listed in previous lessons, or a text of your choice

MATERIALS FOR STUDENTS

- Typed copy of a page from *Spirit of Endurance* (or whatever text you've chosen) without paragraphing
- Pencils
- Document camera

TIME: 45 minutes to 1 hour

Here's How It Goes

"I've read some of *Spirit of Endurance* to you, and today I have a typed page from the text for you." I pass it out. "What do you notice?"

Kids respond that there are no indentations.

"It looks kind of hard to read, doesn't it? Text is much more appealing when the paragraphs are indented. Your job today is to decide where new paragraphs should begin and *why*—what's the rule? Insert the editing sign for a paragraph where you think a new one begins and then leave tracks in the snow telling me why. You'll work with a partner, so I expect to hear some good discussions. When you think you're done, let me know, and I'll show you the page that has the author's paragraphing and you can compare."

When students have finished, we come back together as a class, and the students discuss where they indicated new paragraphs. We chart the rules they've noticed (dialogue, new main idea, etc.) and look at the original text to see where the author started new paragraphs.

Press Your Advantage

I repeat this lesson with another piece of text or simply encourage students to notice how authors of the nonfiction they're reading create paragraphs. I also link this lesson to our reading workshop and have students notice when authors start new paragraphs in the fiction they're reading independently. This calls attention to dialogue paragraphing, which is a difficult skill for students to master.

When Kids Don't Get It

As I move about the room listening in, I stop by partners who appear to be having difficulty and discuss paragraphing with them. If I have students who cannot read the text independently, I either provide a different text example for them to work on or work with them on the text as a group.

One-to-One

It's obvious Oscar and George are struggling, but they haven't asked for help.

Me: Hi, guys, I see you haven't marked anything yet.

George: We're reading it first.

Me: That's fine. I have a suggestion, though. See how this very first line isn't indented? Do you think you could put a paragraph editing mark there?

Oscar: Oh, yeah—it's the start to the piece.

Me: Right. Why don't you guys start reading it out loud to me and when you think the idea changes, we'll stop and talk. [*Oscar starts to read*.]

George: Wait! They start with what's happening to the boat, then right there they start to talk about what the captain is thinking. Is that what you mean, Mrs. B.—something different happens?

Me: Exactly. Another way is to say that there's a new main idea. Can you guys put a paragraph mark there and leave tracks? Are you set to keep going without me?

Oscar: Okay.

George: It's okay if we're not a hundred percent correct, right?

Me: You're working on noticing, and there's some leeway in paragraphing. Nobody will be a hundred percent correct!

Owning the Lesson

Paragraphs are difficult. Although we can apply a generally accepted formula, studying mentor texts demonstrates that paragraphing varies. Texts need varied paragraph lengths to keep the reader's interest. They don't always start with a topic sentence and end with a conclusion. That's for pedagogues. We need to think beyond that.

What could you lift from this lesson to use in your writing classroom? Does it just pertain to explanatory/informative text? How do your students approach paragraphing? Do they depend on you to tell them "how much" or "how long"? Do they understand *why* authors use paragraphs? Are they being intentional with their paragraphing?

Questions to Think About

- Do I ask my students to notice and name how authors construct paragraphs? Can my students articulate *why* an author might have chosen to begin a new paragraph (dialogue, new main idea, new thinking, new action, etc.)?
- Do I push my students beyond formulaic paragraphing?
- Do I teach paragraphing explicitly?

Writing Leads

Introduction

Writers of nonfiction need to grab the reader's attention just like writers of fiction do. Because we have studied and discussed effective leads in the unit on writing fiction, students have those anchor charts to refer to. We spend one class period writing at least two different leads that work for our topic. The next day students share these leads with a partner, get feedback, and create the lead they will use.

MATERIALS FOR STUDENTS

- A lead chosen from material the student has been exploring
- Inquiry notebook

TIME: 45 minutes

CCSS, GRADE BY GRADE

Third graders introduce a topic, group related information together, and include illustrations when they help comprehension.

Fourth graders introduce a topic clearly, group related information in paragraphs and sections, and include formatting (e.g., headings) and illustrations when they help comprehension.

Fifth graders do everything required of a fourth grader and provide more specific observations and focus.

Sixth graders provide more sophisticated introductions and organize ideas, concepts, and information using strategies such as definition, classification, comparison/contrast, cause/effect, formatting (e.g., headings), and graphics (e.g., charts, tables) to help comprehension.

Here's How It Goes

"Here's another chance to go back to our work on noticing leads. Remember how we all used books on our topic to create a chart of great leads? You get to decide how you want to start your piece. Do you want to start with a question? By setting the scene? With dialogue? What's most important or interesting about your topic? Let's take a minute and skim back through our notes to see what might work."

After students have skimmed their notes, I continue, "Today I'd like you to write two different leads. What I really mean is an entire lead paragraph. Try one way and then try an entirely different paragraph. That way when we confer tomorrow, you can make your choice. If you want to try more than two, feel free."

After a bit of discussion, students work independently on their writing and I move around the room and confer.

Press Your Advantage

The following day, students confer with a partner about the leads they've written, deciding which lead is stronger and how they might revise it. Many students combine their two leads into one or write a brand new one. That's the beauty of writing!

When Kids Don't Get It

Creating a great lead can be tough. When students struggle, I show them explicit examples from mentor texts, they choose the one they like, and together we try to mirror it.

One-to-One

I sit down to confer with Hays.

> **Me:** How do you like your lead?
>
> **Hays:** It's okay. I started at the beginning…
>
> **Me:** Go on.
>
> **Hays:** I started with, "Al Capone was born on…"
>
> **Me:** A few biographies start that way. As you were researching, did you find any with that lead?
>
> **Hays:** No, but I've seen others like that.
>
> **Me:** Did you enjoy the writing in those?

Hays: Not so much. Boring.

Me: I'm thinking that Al Capone was quite a character. He must have been if you've stuck with the research on him. I'm also betting we can find a catchier way for you to grab your reader. Tell me why you chose him and maybe what was most interesting to you.

Hays [*after recounting some information about Al Capone*]: He was one bad dude!

Me [*laughing*]: Hays, that sounds so like you!

Hays: Could I start that way? That Al Capone was one bad dude and explain a little in my lead, then do the rest?

Me: What do you think?

Hays: I think I like that better than when he was born.

Owning the Lesson

How often do you ask students to use mentor texts to inform their writing? Typical reports or research papers all start the same. In *Nonfiction Matters* Stephanie Harvey (1998) calls them the cure for insomnia. Boring. Students need to notice what catches their attention and replicate that.

All leads in explanatory/informative text don't need to be the same. What is your purpose? What are your expectations for the students? How does this lesson relate to the lesson on leads for fiction? Does noticing leads transfer to other genres and content areas? Do purposes and leads change for different genres and different audiences?

Questions to Think About

- Is a lead the same as or different from a topic sentence? How are they the same or different?
- Who is in charge of creating leads in my classroom? Is there a set formula or do I allow students to create their own?
- Are my students aware that leads change with genre, purpose, and audience?
- Do mentor texts influence how my students craft leads?
- Have my students encountered enough different kinds of leads to be able to choose one that works best for their piece?

Organizing Ideas

Introduction

When I was in school, I used to worry that someday a teacher would ask me to turn in an outline *before* I wrote the piece. I'd have my information in a basic sequence before I started writing, but I never knew the minutiae, and things always changed. My outline was always written *after* my piece was completed, so that it matched the report. In this lesson I just want to teach kids to be deliberate about the order or sequence of their piece. (If my students are more sophisticated writers, I might include transitions as part of the lesson.)

MENTOR TEXTS FOR STUDENTS

- The mentor texts on which the student pieces are patterned

MATERIALS FOR STUDENTS

- Mentor text on which their piece is based
- Inquiry notebook
- Highlighters

TIME: 30 to 45 minutes

Here's How It Goes

I have written on the board: *Today you will organize your notes. Go through all the questions and number (in a bright color so the numbers stand out) the order that you want to put them in when you write your piece. Each question will turn into a minimum of one paragraph.*

"What order makes sense to you? After your lead what do you think would make the most sense to write about next? Each one of your questions with the notes under them will turn into a paragraph. You might have more than one paragraph for the question, and that's okay. So what is the minimum amount of paragraphs you'll have in your piece?"

I see kids counting mentally. Emma raises her hand. "Seven. The lead, then the five questions, and then the conclusion or ending."

I ask for a student to volunteer her or his notes as an example. I place the notes on the document camera and determine a sequence. Then I ask them to take their own notes and use a colored pen or Sharpie to put a number at the top of each page to show the order.

Interestingly, kids often end up spread out on the floor. There's a natural inclination to share their thought processes with neighbors, to verbalize their intent and rationale for which questions should come in which order.

Press Your Advantage

Students are ready to write. I have students leave their notebooks open on their tables when they leave for the evening, so I can double-check their sequencing. Can they change their sequence while they're writing? Absolutely. That's part of the process.

When Kids Don't Get It

As I check the students' sequences, I list students who need to revisit the lesson. I work with them individually (or in a small group) the next day while everyone else works on his or her draft independently.

One-to-One

Trinity is working independently, but she had requested a conference during my status check at the beginning of the period.

Trinity: I've been working on my Alcatraz piece, but I don't think I like the way I planned it out.

Me: Go on.

Trinity: Well, see how I ordered my notes? Now I'm thinking that it doesn't make sense to go in that order. I think I'd rather write about this question first. Can I move things around?

Me: What do you think? You're the writer—if you move the order of these questions, will it make your piece better?

Trinity: Yes.

Me: Then before you continue writing take another-color pen and renumber your notes, so that both you and I know the new order.

Trinity: Okay.

Owning the Lesson

Writing is messy, and authors are often surprised when a draft takes them somewhere they didn't expect. However, it helps students to have a sequence in mind when writing explanatory/informative text. They need to know where they're starting and where they're heading—they need a plan. (That doesn't mean they can't change their mind.)

Because my students' notes are all in their inquiry notebook, using a pen to number the order makes sense. If your students have used note cards, they can lay them out and then number them. Or they could create a storyboard or other graphic organizer. There is no one way to do this. The important thing is that students are choosing the sequence, not following a preset form.

What works for you when you write explanatory/informative text? How could you share that process with your students? Is there only one way to sequence? Can you offer students options? Know your students, their needs, and their learning styles.

Questions to Think About

- How does organizing ideas differ from creating an outline?
- Am I in charge of sequencing the writing, or are my students?
- How else could students plan their sequence? How do my students use their peers and me to determine whether their plan makes sense?
- How do my students change their sequence once they begin to draft if they need to?

- How often do I use conferences, both with peers and with me, to give ample feedback to my writers?

- How do I ensure that my students are exposed to a wide variety of mentor texts and discuss different organizational styles and formats *before* they begin writing?

Drafting, Editing, and Revising

Introduction

My students do a lot of writing both in school and at home, and most of them receive feedback and suggestions from peers and family members, and all receive it from me. Sometimes I want an authentic assessment of their writing, writing they do in class without input from home. I use these nonfiction pieces for this in-class assessment. Students read and take notes at school and at home, but once we start drafting, they can't take their rough drafts home until they are complete and I've checked them. If students have word processed the draft, they print off a copy and I write my editor's comments directly on the hard copy. Although we've conferred throughout the process, I want them to experience an editor's notes and comments and go back and revise. Students also confer with their classmates along the way, but I'm the final editor. Figure 4.11 is a copy of a student's draft with my revision comments.

MENTOR TEXTS FOR TEACHERS

Here are some resources that go into detail about the writing process:

- Jim Burke's *What's the Big Idea? Question-Driven Units to Motivate Reading, Writing, and Thinking* (2010)

- Ruth Culham's *Traits of Writing: The Complete Guide for Middle School* (2010)

- Katie Wood Ray's *The Writing Workshop: Working Through the Hard Parts (and They're All Hard Parts)* (2001) and *Study Driven: A Framework for Planning Units of Study in the Writing Workshop* (2006)

Figure 4.11 I write directly on the student's draft, asking questions and generally pushing for more. I act like a professional editor would. However, I am careful with what I write: Our words have power! I want to improve the writing without noting the negatives. If there is something glaring, I'll have a conference with the student to discuss what I notice instead of writing about it in the margins.

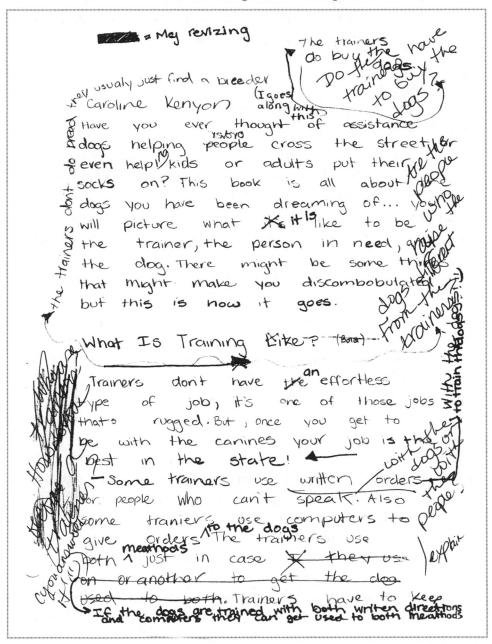

MATERIALS FOR STUDENTS

- Mentor text on which their piece is based
- Writer's notebook/loose-leaf paper/folders/word processor (some students prefer to write in their notebook, others don't want to flip back and forth and use loose-leaf paper or another notebook)

TIME: two weeks of writing workshop sessions

Here's How It Goes

This lesson builds on the foundational work of setting up the writing process in Lesson Cluster One. If students are drafting, revising, and editing independently, these two weeks are truly a workshop. My job is to get out of the way and let students write. (I also confer, confer, confer; teach, teach, teach; and *learn, learn, learn*). If you walked into the room, you'd have to look very hard to find me; I'm a writer among writers.

Up to this point, I've been conducting minilessons and teaching explicitly. Now that the groundwork has been laid, I can release students to work independently. At the beginning of each day's writing workshop, I take a status check so I know where each child is in the process and who needs a conference. Then I circulate, checking how the students are incorporating their notes into their drafts. Many times students realize they don't have enough information on a particular section of their topic. The solution is to go back and take more notes. Having two weeks to write allows students to dig in and do their best work and allows me to help them do that.

I always address plagiarism earlier, when we take notes. If I notice students copying verbatim from texts, I make them change it then, so it's not a temptation to plagiarize when writing. If a student wants to insert a quote, I teach him or her how—as well as how to reference it—and we use the document camera to show the rest of the class what that looks like.

Students may finalize their draft at home, but they must turn in both their rough draft and their final draft (that way, obvious inconsistencies are apparent). Because we spend at least two weeks writing every day and I'm conferring with the students regularly, I know their pieces practically by heart. Our classroom has laptop computers, so many students word process their drafts, in which case they can send their rough draft home as an email attachment (the era before computers is a distant memory!). They often end up embedding photographs and diagrams.

Some students prefer to handwrite their rough drafts in class and word process the final versions at home.

We also build in time each day for students to confer with classmates.

Press Your Advantage

Some kids rush through and finish their drafts early, but because they get them back with comments almost immediately, they're the ones who end up spending more time revising. Students who revise as they draft take longer but receive fewer comments and suggestions from me. Once I've checked their draft, they're usually set to move on to editing.

To extend this lesson, you might have students begin working on their oral presentation. Sometimes I have students capture the salient points of their topic in a poem (see Figure 4.12) and include it as part of their article. Alternatively, students always have ongoing writing projects and independent reading to return to.

When Kids Don't Get It

When students are having difficulty at this stage, I need to work with them individually.

One-to-One

Ben brings me his rough draft of his piece on Jack Nicklaus.

>**Ben:** I think I'm done with my draft.
>
>**Me:** You have been working so hard. Have you enjoyed the writing?
>
>**Ben:** Yeah, and I've learned a lot. You know how I like to study athletes.
>
>**Me:** And you know I'm not a golfer! When I read your piece, am I going to understand it? If I didn't know who Jack Nicklaus was, would I understand why he's important right from the start?
>
>**Ben:** Well, I know about him.
>
>**Me:** Yep, but you're the researcher! Before you turn your paper in for me to read, revise, and comment on, I'd like you to go back through and read it with a *reader's eyes* and see if you've explained it well. Maybe mark places where you might need a little more explanation, and then I'll come back and we can work on those. How's that sound?

Ben is already at work.

Figure 4.12 Student Poem Based on Research

LEGO

WHEN THE FIRST
BRICK CAME OUT
THE ONLY SOUND
THE OWNER HEARD
WAS THE LOVELY
CHA-CHING!
WHEN DUPLO
CAME OUT
THE LEGO GROUP
BECAME BIGGER
WITH BIGGER BRICKS
AND BUNNY HEADS,
WOODEN TOOLS AND TOYS
NO MORE.
LATER WHEN MINDSTORMS CAME
THE ROBOTS YELLED, "BUY ME!"
AND MADE A TYCOON
COMPANY.

Owning the Lesson

Is your writing workshop set up so that students understand the writing process and can work through a piece or project independently? How do you view your role during this time? Are you able to meet with small groups or individuals as the rest of the students are working? How will you monitor what your students are working on, where they are in the process, and how they use their time? What are your students' needs and abilities? How much time will they need to draft and complete the article? Will it be finalized in class or at home? Be sure you slice all these pieces of the pie as you're setting up this research unit.

Could you take aspects of this lesson and apply them to other content areas and other types of explanatory/informative writing? This lesson can scaffold or piggyback on other writing across the curriculum.

Questions to Think About

- How does having a plan already formulated help my students begin to work independently?

- How are my students using mentor texts to guide their writing? How do I know that? Through individual conferences or through the reflections I ask them to write?

- Do my students have enough information in their notes? If not, how do I help them get more?

- How do I decide whether students have enough time to work through the writing process in depth without being rushed? If I haven't budgeted enough time, is my day flexible enough that I can find the additional time my students need?

- How do I monitor deadlines and support students who aren't able to meet these deadlines?

- How often do my students get input and feedback from peers and from me to improve and enhance their writing?

Presenting and Sharing Students' Texts and Knowledge

Introduction

In addition to celebrating their final written pieces, I allow a week for my students to give oral presentations on their topic so they can practice their speaking skills. Each student has a maximum of twenty minutes to set up, present, and answer questions. Parents are welcome to attend. This is one of our favorite weeks—we learn so much from one another!

MATERIALS FOR STUDENTS

- Final draft
- Book lover's book

TIME: 1 week

Here's How It Goes

The day all written pieces are turned in, students place their work on their tables, then walk about the room, reading and enjoying their classmates' writing. There is absolutely no talking, and pieces may be read by only one person at a time. After everyone has read all the pieces, students talk with and congratulate one another. All the pieces are then displayed in the hall under a Meet the Researchers banner for everyone in the school to read. (That's why they need to be perfect!) I mount them on twelve-by-eighteen-inch construction paper with each child's name at the bottom. (It helps to type the name and laminate each page.)

I also have students reflect on the process and how it went in their book lover's book. This part is incredibly important. It solidifies their learning. It's also an opportunity for them to give me advice or offer suggestions. I take what they say to heart—their input makes me a better teacher.

The oral presentations need to be different from the written pieces—students can't just stand up and read them. They decide how they want to present their information. Some turn the article into a PowerPoint presentation. Others will dress up as the character and role-play. Todd researched and wrote an article about Nintendo, then dressed as Mario to share what he had learned. Riley, ever the actress, speaking as an inmate at Alcatraz, told us what it was like to be locked up there. Connor built a replica of the Golden Gate Bridge; Sydney used links to the Internet to play videos of swans and their different cries. Some students create posters. Anything goes as long as it enhances the presentation. Parents are invited to come in and watch, learn from the experts. I send home a sheet ahead of time with the presentation times and topics.

I score these presentations using a district speaking rubric, but I don't grade the visual aids. I want my students' time and effort directed to their oral presentation skills. I used to have the other students take notes on the presentations so I could evaluate how well they listened, but it took away from their enjoyment of what their classmates were saying. Now I allow time at the end of each presentation for questions and evaluate their listening that way.

Pressing Your Advantage

Many times a student's research encourages other students to find out more. When Micha researched Down syndrome, many students wanted to find out more so they could understand students in our school with Down syndrome. When Geoffrey told us about Jesse Owens at the Olympics and Madison taught us about the horrors in World War II internment camps, the class wanted to know more about the Nazis, and we found read-aloud books and book club books to help us do that. This unit allows students to learn about twenty-five topics (give or take, depending on the number of students in your class) they probably wouldn't have been exposed to in a traditional curriculum. Even better, students learn *how* to research and *access* new knowledge. Think of the power in that!

When Kids Don't Get It

If I've done my job, they should have. We draft in class, so I know they have a product. That's another reason I depend on my conferences during the two weeks student are writing—I need to check their progress. If students are unable to finalize at home, I find a way for them to get it done at school.

One-on-One

This is time to celebrate! The one-on-one here takes place as students interact with one another. They congratulate one another for phenomenally written pieces. They ask one another thoughtful questions. They discuss what they've learned from one another. I also relate one-on-one with the reflections my students have written, thinking about my instruction and how I can improve and can help my students be even more successful.

Owning the Lesson

You don't have to do everything in this lesson. There are so many components—sharing written pieces, giving oral presentations, reflecting. What is your purpose, what are you assessing, how much time do you have? I use the research process and project to teach and assess all the literacy standards—reading, writing, language, speaking, and listening. That doesn't mean you have to. Which aspects of this lesson or this lesson cluster are manageable for you? What could you pull from these lessons and tweak to fit your teaching style, grade level, and curriculum?

Questions to Think About

- How is my students' writing celebrated and made public?
- How do my students reflect on their learning and their process?
- How do I ensure that my students understand the value of reflecting, that it helps them as students and helps me inform my teaching?
- Do I provide my students opportunities to demonstrate what they've learned in varied ways?
- Do my students understand how they will be assessed and receive feedback? What type of feedback do they receive and what do they do with it?

Wrap-Up

The CCSS ensure that nonfiction (informative/explanatory) text will be playing a bigger role in our classrooms. With students now expected to be reading informative/explanatory text 50 percent of the time and one-third of the writing standards focusing on writing informative text, the genre has a prominent place at the table. Luckily, there are so many wonderful texts available, at a variety of difficulty levels. We don't have to depend only on textbooks to meet these standards.

My students invariably rank the research unit as one of their favorite parts of the year. At the end of each year I ask students to reflect on what helped them most to grow as readers, as writers, as mathematicians. Research is always high on the list. Conferring is right up there, too. When students come back to visit, they always mention the research projects. Most say they still have their final products! Todd, now graduating from college, emailed me and asked whether I remember when he dressed up as Mario for his Nintendo project. Of course I do!

Why is this so memorable—and powerful? Choice. Passion. Interest. The chance to dig in deeply. Students own their research. I give them guidelines, expectations, and a foundation, but they own the product. And they learn so much from their peers, more than I could begin to teach in a year.

They also learn *how* to access information. They know how to ask great questions. They know how to find answers. And they have foundational skills that will last a lifetime: determining importance in text, taking notes, drafting, using models for their own writing, speaking in front of an audience. Think of how many adults you know who are petrified to get up in front of people!

I started teaching the research process in my classroom long before the CCSS made their debut. Authentic research was my purpose. When I read the CCSS, I was thrilled to see that my approach meshed with their expectations, that I could use the research process to help my students meet so many of the individual standards.

Think about the standards in relation to your curriculum and your students. What aspects of these lessons could you try? You don't have to do it all—begin with one lesson from this cluster. And adapt the lessons to fit your purpose. Each time I introduce the research process to my students, I change the unit a bit—add more here, streamline there—to best achieve what I set out to accomplish.

What About Assessment?

I assess students throughout these lessons. I always ask students to reflect on their process and product. I often have them set goals for their next research project.

Rubrics are essential assessment tools. I also keep anecdotal notes on informal assessments. I use a six-traits writing rubric to assess students' final nonfiction piece and a speaking rubric for their oral presentation. One caution: We can "over-rubric" our kids to the point that all they see is a number. Although I attach a number ranking to my assessment, my students are more interested in the comments I write. They have been immersed in a project for many weeks, and they deserve detailed feedback on how I viewed their use of class time, their growth, and their final product. Words have power. I choose mine carefully, and I focus on the positive. If I've done my job well, I've given each student the knowledge and encouragement they need.

What Else?

These lessons build on those in Lesson Cluster One dealing with writing president paragraphs and setting up the writing workshop so that students write independently with stamina over extended periods of time. They build on those in Lesson Cluster Two in which students dig into vocabulary and language and use mentor texts.

Learning from peers instead of from a textbook or a lecture is a powerful concept. What else could you do with this research framework? Could you use it to dig deeply into a science topic? Investigate a social studies topic? Divide and conquer a period of history? How else could you incorporate technology? There are so many other possibilities.

If your interest is piqued, be a researcher and delve into one of the mentor texts for teachers I've highlighted—each has a different slant, a different flavor, but they all focus on authenticity and student ownership.

Things to Think About

- How much informative/explanatory text do I currently have in my classroom? Do I use it in reading instruction? Writing instruction? Do I need more? How much more?

- Which lessons from this section intrigue me and meet my students' needs—and my assessment requirements?

- How can I introduce the research process into my classroom? Could I start small, then build?

- How can I use the concept of mentor texts to enhance writing instruction on informative/explanatory texts?

- Finally, what is my *purpose*?

Afterword

I'll share a secret. Authors often wait until they finish a book to write the introduction—and only then can they write the conclusion. That way, they are sure to bookend the material in between. That's what I've done here—the book is written, I just finished the introduction, and now I need to wrap it up. As my students well know, endings are tough. When I wrote *The Inside Guide to the Reading–Writing Classroom*, I surrounded myself with mentor texts. I did so again this time. I wanted to see how the authors of other lesson books wrap it up. I discovered that many don't! The last chapter ends and the appendix begins. But I invited you to sit by me as we walked through the lessons together, and I want to end by handing the lessons over to you to make your own. It's your turn.

To be honest, this book began with Maddie walking several classroom visitors through my students' writing process. I knew she had to lead you into the book as well. Her comment, "We study mentor texts a lot, and we do reading and writing together," encapsulates the advice I want to give.

I hope I've provided you with enough mentor texts to get started. I hope that I've acted as a mentor for you. Maddie unequivocally knows the power that writing has given her. All my students know that—that's why they want to share. And I want to add that writing goes beyond the Common Core State Standards. Yes, the standards are a reality in our lives as educators, but I want my students to learn to write authentically—to notice how authors use words, to have power over the written word, to communicate, to think. If I give them that, I know it will transfer to any testing situation.

I'm passing these lessons on to you. It's your turn to be choosey. Time for you to read and write along with your students. I hope you return to these lessons time and again, continuing to add and tweak and press your advantage. My hope is that when visitors enter your classroom, your students can lead them through their writing process the way Maddie did. That when students reflect, they know the joy of both reading and writing a well-written text. Because standards come and go, and the pendulum swings, but the one thing that always remains constant is great writing—and what a gift that is!

Editing Timeline

I include grammar and mechanics when I plan the year. On this chart are three columns—mechanics, grammar, and assessments. I begin with the assessments before adding the specifics. I start with state testing and then work backward, making sure I have provided direct instruction on all components of the test and everything measured on the standards. Once I have taught and students have practiced a skill, I hold them accountable for using it correctly in *all* their written work. I evaluate how they are doing through informal assessments and their scores on the "Conventions" section of the six-traits record chart.

Week	Grammar	Mechanics	Assessments/Reporting, etc.
1	Getting to know the kids!		
2		Capitals	
3			
4		Endmarks Periods	
5	Nouns – verbs –		
6			INFORMAL ASSESSMENTS
7		Commas	Assessment Also Monitored
8			by Scoring the Conventions
9	Pronouns		Section of 6-Trait Rubric –
10		Dialogue Question Marks	Authentic Use
11			
12	Adjectives		
13			
14		Review Paragraphs Apostrophes	
15	Adverbs	Reinforcing	
16			
17			
18			
19	Using Grammar in Meaningful Ways		
20			
21			

22		Study on Punctuation- Use in Authentic Ways	Review/ Practice For State/ National Assessments
23			
24			
25	Using/Identifying Grammar Authentically		
26			
27			↕ State Assess (standards)
28			
29			
30			
31		Use of Punctuation Correctly in Written Work (Authenticity!)	
32			
33			Continue to Informally Assess
34			
35			
36			
37			
38			

Appendix B

Revision Timeline

I also plan my instruction in the skills students need to revise their writing. The first column of this chart focuses on the six traits of writing. Although the six traits are not part of the writing process as such, I want my students to understand each trait and to see how using it improves writing. I start the year with word choice, as words give writing power; I also want students to notice vocabulary, and the two are entwined. The second column, "Language," includes figurative language. Once we have studied how published authors use figurative language, I have my students practice using it in their writing, especially their president paragraphs. By the time students take the state assessments, they have had ample practice using figurative language in their own writing. The final column, "Assessments/ Projects," itemizes tests and writing projects. Again, I put this on the chart before I add anything else, and then work backward. I want to make sure I have taught everything that will be assessed on formal tests prior to the test. You will notice that much of the third column is covered by "informal assessments" and scores on each trait of the six-traits rubric. That is how I measure student progress. At the end of the year, I do a unit of study on revision to allow students to practice everything we've worked on, as a form of assessment.

Week	6-Trait Focus	Language	Assessments/Projects
1	Introducing Paragraphing		
2	Organi-zation		DRA = Testing NWEA Maps Testing
3		Onomatopoeia	
4		Alliteration	
5	WORD CHOICE	Simile	
6			
7		Personification	Rubric
8			
9	Ideas and Content	Metaphor	
10			
11			
12		Hyperbole	Assessing Based on the Students Writing and 6-Trait Rubric
13			
14	Sentence Fluency		
15			
16			
17		Noticing How Authors Use Language & Sentences to Create Voice	
18			
19	Voice		
20			
21			

22	Focus on Conventions - Using Them Authentically	Purpose/ Audience Testing as a Genre	Study on Punctuation
23			
24			End Trimester
25			
26			
27			State Testing
28			
29			
30			
31			
32			Unit of Study on Revision - Revising a Prior Piece
33			
34			
35			
36			NWEA Maps Testing
37			
38			

Appendix C

Record Sheets

These record sheets document individual students' proficiency with elements of the six traits of writing (which coincide with portions of the Common Core State Standards). Although I could use them with all student writing, I save them for finalized pieces.

I divide the sheet for *editing skills* into trimesters, focusing on specific skills during each one. I record the student's writing pieces and indicate "proficiency" or "needs support." Based on progress, I reteach concepts to the whole class or provide small-group instruction.

The sheet for *word choice* encompasses figurative language and using specific words. I don't expect students to use all types of figurative language in every piece, but this sheet helps me track which ones students are using independently in their writing.

Two more sheets track the remaining traits—*organization, ideas and content, sentence fluency*, and *voice*—including specific subcategories. I record a numerical score (0–5, with 0 indicating that students did not attempt to use the trait and 5 indicating an advanced score), then check the skills the student demonstrates.

Combined, these record-keeping charts allow me to follow each student's progress and are invaluable when completing achievement records and holding parent conferences.

									Name _____ Writing Piece/date
									ORGANIZATION –SCORE
									–Beginning, middle and end
									–Lead or topic sentence
									–Transitions
									–Strong conclusion
									–IDEAS & CONTENT –SCORE
									–Strong focus/ main idea
									–Details
									6-Trait/ Language Record Sheet Comment

Name _____

6-Trait/Language Record Sheet

Writing Piece/date									
SENTENCE FLUENCY–SCORE									
–Complete									
–Variety of beginnings									
–Clauses									
Complex/compound									
Other									
VOICE– SCORE									
Comments									

Writing Piece/date										Name
										+ = demonstrates proficiency
										– = needs support
									Subject/ verb agreement	↑
									Complete sentences	
									Endmarks	Fri. 1
									Capitalization	
									Spelling	↓
									Paragraphing	↑
									Commas	
									Dialogue	Fri. 2
									Quotation marks	↓
									Other– Parentheses	↑ Fri. 3
									Ellipses, dashes, hyphens	↓
									Comments	Editing Record Chart

Works Cited

Blauman, Leslie. 2011. *The Inside Guide to the Reading–Writing Classroom: Strategies for Extraordinary Teaching.* Portsmouth, NH: Heinemann.

Bomer, Katherine. 2010. *Hidden Gems.* Portsmouth, NH: Heinemann.

Burke, Jim. 2010. *What's the Big Idea? Question-Driven Units to Motivate Reading, Writing, and Thinking.* Portsmouth, NH: Heinemann.

Culham, Ruth. 2010. *Traits of Writing: The Complete Guide for Middle School.* New York: Scholastic.

Daniels, Harvey, and Stephanie Harvey. 2009. *Comprehension and Collaboration: Inquiry Circles in Action.* Portsmouth, NH: Heinemann.

———. 2011. *Texts and Lessons for Content-Area Reading.* Portsmouth, NH: Heinemann.

Daniels, Harvey, and Steven Zemelman. 2004. *Subjects Matter: Every Teacher's Guide to Content-Area Reading.* Portsmouth, NH: Heinemann.

Daniels, Harvey, Steven Zemelman, and Nancy Steineke. 2007. *Content-Area Writing, Every Teacher's Guide.* Portsmouth, NH: Heinemann.

Davis, Judy, and Sharon Hill. 2003. *The No-Nonsense Guide to Teaching Writing: Strategies, Structures, and Solutions.* Portsmouth, NH: Heinemann.

Fletcher, Ralph. 1996. *A Writer's Notebook: Unlocking the Writer Within You.* New York: HarperCollins.

———. 1999. *Live Writing: Breathing Life into Your Words.* New York: HarperCollins.

———. 2000. *How Writers Work: Finding a Process That Works for You.* New York: Harper Collins.

———. 2002. *Poetry Matters: Writing a Poem from the Inside Out.* New York: Harper Trophy.

———. 2006. *Boy Writers: Reclaiming Their Voices.* Portland, ME: Stenhouse.

Fletcher, Ralph, and Joann Portalupi. 2001. *Nonfiction Craft Lessons.* Portland, ME: Stenhouse.

———. 2001. *Writing Workshop: The Essential Guide.* Portsmouth, NH: Heinemann.

Goldberg, Natalie. 2010. *Writing Down the Bones.* Expanded ed. Boston, MA: Shambhala.

Graves, Donald. 1989. *Experiment with Fiction.* Part of the Reading/Writing Teacher's Companion series. Portsmouth, NH: Heinemann.

———. 1992. *Explore Poetry.* Portsmouth, NH: Heinemann.

———. 1994. *A Fresh Look at Writing.* Portsmouth, NH: Heinemann.

Harvey, Stephanie. 1998. *Nonfiction Matters.* Portland, ME: Stenhouse.

Harvey, Stephanie, and Anne Goudvis. 2000. *Strategies That Work*. Portland, ME: Stenhouse.

Harwayne, Shelley. 2001. *Writing Through Childhood: Rethinking Process and Product.* Portsmouth, NH: Heinemann.

Heard, Georgia. 1989. *For the Good of the Sun and the Earth: Teaching Poetry.* Portsmouth, NH: Heinemann.

Hyerle, David, and Chris Yeager. 2007. *Thinking Maps, A Language for Learning.* Cary, North Carolina: Thinking Maps, Inc.

Jones, Stephen R., and Ruth Carol Cushman. 1998. *A Month-By-Month Guide to Wildlife and Wild Places. Colorado Nature Almanac*. Boulder, CO: Pruett Publishing Co.

Lane, Barry. 1993. *After the End.* Portsmouth, NH: Heinemann.

———. 1999. *The Reviser's Toolbox.* Shoreham, VT: Discover Writing Press.

———. 2001. *Why We Must Run with Scissors.* Shoreham, VT: Discover Writing Press.

Lintor Make-A-Book products. Available at: www.lintorpublishing.com/default.php.

Nagy, William E. 1988. *Teaching Vocabulary to Improve Reading Comprehension.* Newark, DE: International Reading Association.

Overmeyer, Mark. 2005. *When Writer's Workshop Isn't Working*. Portland, ME: Stenhouse.

Ray, Katie Wood. 1999. *Wondrous Words.* Urbana, IL: National Council of Teachers of English.

———. 2001. *The Writing Workshop: Working Through the Hard Parts (and They're All Hard Parts).* Urbana, IL: National Council of Teachers of English.

———. 2006. *Study Driven: A Framework for Planning Units of Study in the Writing Workshop.* Portsmouth, NH: Heinemann.

Rief, Linda. 2007. *Inside the Writer's-Reader's Notebook: A Workshop Essential.* Portsmouth, NH: Heinemann.

Routman, Regie. 2000. *Kids' Poems: Teaching Third and Fourth Graders to Love Writing Poetry*. New York: Scholastic.

StoryJumper. Available at: www.storyjumper.com.

Spandel, Vicki. 2000. *Creating Writers Through 6-Trait Writing Assessment and Instruction.* New York: Addison Wesley Longmont.

Truss, Lynne. 2006. *Eats, Shoots, and Leaves*. New York: Gotham Books.

Index

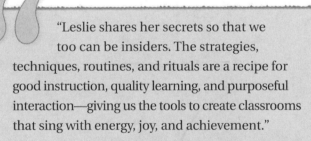